Philip King

Chromebooks

covers all models of Chromebooks

Chrome OS for all ages!

In easy steps is an imprint of In Easy Steps Limited
16 Hamilton Terrace · Holly Walk · Leamington Spa
Warwickshire · United Kingdom · CV32 4LY
www.ineasysteps.com

Notice of Liability
Every effort has been made to ensure that this book contains accurate
and current information. However, In Easy Steps Limited and the
author shall not be liable for any loss or damage suffered by readers
as a result of any information contained herein.

Trademarks
All trademarks are acknowledged as belonging to their respective
companies.

In Easy Steps Limited supports The Forest Stewardship Council (FSC),
the leading international forest certification organization. All our titles
that are printed on Greenpeace approved FSC certified paper carry the
FSC logo.

MIX
Paper from
responsible sources
FSC® C020837

Printed and bound in the United Kingdom

ISBN 978-1-84078-958-4

Contents

11 Video Calling

12 Casting and Connecting

13 Maintenance and Troubleshooting

1 Introducing Chromebooks

Chromebooks are becoming ever more popular as low-cost laptops, with some even able to double up as tablets. This chapter gives an overview of what a Chromebook is, its unique Chrome OS operating system, and how to choose which model to buy.

What is a Chromebook?

A Chromebook is a laptop computer that runs the Chrome OS operating system – rather than Windows, macOS, or Linux. Chrome OS is made by Google and is based around its popular Chrome web browser.

The Chromebook format was first introduced by Google in 2011. While a few people were highly skeptical at the time, it has proven extremely successful. In 2020, over 30 million Chromebooks were sold worldwide – that's more than the total sales of all Apple Mac computers in the same year. Due to the relatively low price of entry-level models, they are particularly popular in educational settings: by 2018, around 60% of all computers purchased by US schools were Chromebooks.

While Google itself now produces its own Pixelbook range (and, previously, the Chromebook Pixel), most Chromebooks are made by other manufacturers, including well-known companies such as Samsung, HP, Lenovo, Acer, and ASUS.

ASUS Chromebook Flip CX5
Image © ASUS

What are the advantages?
If you use your computer mainly for email, general web surfing, and social media platforms such as Facebook, then a Chromebook is an excellent choice. The primary advantages are:

- **Price**. For comparable processing power and performance, Chromebooks are notably cheaper than their Windows counterparts, while Apple MacBooks are considerably more expensive.
- **Security**. Chromebooks are defended from malware by multiple layers of protection. Each web page and application

Beware

It can take a little time to get used to Chrome OS after using Windows or macOS.

runs in a "sandboxed" environment to contain any threat and prevent it from accessing the rest of the computer. Data in the cloud (see below) and stored locally is also very well encrypted. In addition, by default, Chrome OS will receive regular updates automatically to counter any new threats that appear.

- **Speed**. A Chromebook can start up and be ready to use in seconds. This is due to the lightweight nature of the Chrome OS operating system and the fast SSD (solid-state drive) storage that, unlike a hard drive, doesn't have any moving parts.
- **Battery**. Typically, a Chromebook can be used for a full eight-hour working day (or even longer) without needing a recharge from the mains adaptor.
- **Sync**. The data from all your Google apps is synced in the cloud, so you can access it in a browser (when signed in to your account) on another device, or in the same apps on an Android smartphone.
- **Android apps**. Modern Chromebooks can also run the vast range of Android smartphone apps and games. While they are usable with the touchpad and keyboard, they work best with a touchscreen. Some Chromebooks can even be transformed into a touchscreen tablet device by flipping the screen around.

Cloud computing

Although it is possible to use many applications and access files offline, Chromebooks are designed to be used mainly online. This is known as "cloud computing". After logging in with your Google account, you will have full access to your own personal cloud.

As well as containing your files in Google Drive (which can easily be shared with colleagues and others to collaborate on) and photos in Google Photos, your personal cloud is based around a range of core office and productivity applications. Accessed in the Chrome web browser, these include Gmail for sending and receiving email, Calendar for your appointments and reminders, Keep for your notes, and a trio of office applications: Google Docs (for word processing), Sheets (spreadsheets), and Slides (presentations). Read more about these in Chapter 8.

You'll need a wireless connection to the internet via Wi-Fi to use your Chromebook online.

Your Chromebook saves your most recently opened office documents so that you can work on them offline.

Hot tip

If you just want to browse the web and use Google office apps (Google Workspace apps), an entry-level Chromebook may well suffice.

Choosing a Chromebook

Just like Windows laptops, Chromebooks come in a variety of sizes and form factors, from numerous manufacturers.

While standard entry-level Chromebook models are comparatively inexpensive compared to similar Windows computers, there are also "Plus" and "Premium" range models that add extra features and processing power and can cost over $1,000/£1,000.

With that in mind, we'll guide you through the major factors involved in choosing a Chromebook model to buy.

Form factor

Chromebooks are available in three main form factors:

- **Standard laptop.** This is the classic "clamshell" laptop design with a hinged screen that folds shut onto the keyboard when not in use. Many Chromebooks employ this style – some with a standard screen, others with

Google Pixelbook Go
Image © Google

a touchscreen. If you want a traditional laptop and aren't that bothered about using it as a touchscreen tablet device, this may well suit you.

Don't forget

Modern Chromebooks can run Android apps downloaded from the Google Play Store, so a touchscreen is preferable.

- **Convertible.** Also known as "2-in-1", this Chromebook form factor is becoming more popular, offering you dual laptop/ tablet functionality. The hinged screen can be

Acer Spin 513
Image © Acer

rotated all the way back and around to the rear of the keyboard section to transform the device into a touchscreen tablet. This is particularly useful if you want to run Android smartphone/ tablet apps and games on it.

- **Detachable**. So far, only a handful of Chromebooks come in this format. A 2-in-1 device, its touchscreen can be detached from the keyboard section to use it on its own as a tablet. Again, this is ideal for running Android smartphone/tablet apps and games, for which you can use an on-screen keyboard for any text input.

Lenovo IdeaPad Duet
Image © Lenovo

Other considerations

Once you've decided which type of Chromebook design you favor, there are some other key aspects to consider:

- **Screen size**. As when choosing any laptop, this is one of the most important factors. While a large screen is often desirable, there's an obvious trade-off with portability. So, if you want something you can slip into a small bag to carry around, you may prefer a smaller display.
- **Screen resolution**. The standard native screen resolution for Chromebooks is 1920 x 1080 pixels. However, some cheaper models may feature a lower resolution; this may be fine on a smaller screen. Some high-end Chromebooks feature a higher resolution, such as the Acer Spin 713 (2256 x 1504 pixels).
- **Processor speed**. The more powerful the processor, the faster the computer will run, in particular when multitasking with several apps. Since Chrome OS is such a lightweight operating system, however, even a lower-end processor may well suffice.
- **RAM**. This is the amount of memory the Chromebook has. Typically, this will be 4GB, but some higher-end models have 8GB or 16GB of RAM. This may be an advantage for heavy multitasking.
- **Storage**. Space for storing your files offline, and Android apps, this is typically 32GB or 64GB on a Chromebook, but can go up to 128GB or 256GB. An SSD is preferable to eMMC (embedded MultiMediaCard) flash.

Hot tip

Always check the Auto Update Expiry (AUE) date for the Chromebook model you are considering. After this, it will no longer receive system software updates from Google.

Don't forget

Because Chrome OS is so lightweight, even a lower-end processor will run things a lot faster on a Chromebook than it would on a Windows PC.

About Chrome OS

Chrome OS is the operating system that runs on Chromebooks. An operating system controls the general operation of a computer and manages all the hardware and other software on it. Other popular operating systems include Windows, macOS, and Linux.

Key differences

Chrome OS is a little different from most other operating systems, as it based around the concept of cloud computing. The latter involves storing and accessing files, data, and programs on remote servers over the internet, instead of them all being stored on your computer's local storage system.

Even so, a Chromebook does include some internal storage in the form of an SSD or eMMC flash, so you can continue to work on files when you have no internet. The amount of storage on a Chromebook will typically be smaller than on a standard laptop as you don't require so much offline storage.

Instead of installing applications locally on the Chromebook, most are typically run as web apps inside the Chrome browser. You can't install Microsoft Office on your Chromebook, for instance, although you can still use the online version of it and also open and edit Microsoft Office documents in the Google Workspace office apps.

The exception to this general rule of web apps is that modern Chromebooks can also run Android apps obtained from the Google Play Store, which are downloaded and installed locally on the computer, just as they would be on an Android smartphone or tablet device. We will explain how this works in Chapter 10.

Core applications

Chrome OS comes with a range of Google's own core applications. These can be found (if installed) in the app Launcher at the bottom of the desktop – drag it up with the touchpad or press the **Everything Button**: ￼ or ￼.

Beware

If you want to continue working on Google office documents when offline, **Offline** mode must be turned **On** in each app's settings.

12

- **Chrome**. Google's popular web browser is the most important application on your Chromebook, as it's used to run all the other standard web apps (i.e. non-Android apps). Read more details about how to use Chrome effectively in Chapter 5.

...cont'd

- **Gmail**. Google's email application enables you to write and send messages from your Google account. You can also easily organize emails into folders and filter spam and junk mail. See Chapter 6 for more details.

- **Google Drive**. This is where all of your files are stored online. It can be accessed from other devices on which you are signed in to your Google account. You can also share selected files and folders with other people, making it easy to collaborate. See Chapter 7 for more details.

- **Files**. Open this app to find all the files stored locally in your Chromebook's SSD storage. It contains default folders for Downloads, Camera (for photos taken by the Chromebook's camera), and Play Files (for Android app files), but you can create your own folders to organize files.

- **Docs**. Google's word processing application has plenty of advanced formatting features. As with the other office apps, documents are stored in Google Drive, with a copy of currently open documents also stored on the Chromebook so that you can continue working when offline. It can also be used to open and edit files in other formats, such as Microsoft Word. See Chapter 8 for more details.

Google office app documents can be shared with others, enabling you all to collaborate and make comments and edits.

- **Sheets**. Google's application for working on spreadsheets offers all the usual features such as formulas, charts, pivot tables, and conditional formatting. It can also be used to edit files in other formats, such as Microsoft Excel.

- **Slides**. Google's application for producing presentations, Slides offers a wide range of themes and fonts to choose from. Advanced features enable you to embed videos and add animations. It can also be used to edit files in other formats, such as Microsoft PowerPoint.

...cont'd

- **Google Duo**. This video- and audio-calling app is free to use. Like WhatsApp, it relies on your mobile phone number for identification purposes and to access your contacts.

- **Google Maps**. If you need to find shops and services in a particular location, the Maps app is a great help. It's also great for planning a journey and giving you directions.

- **YouTube**. The world's most popular video website comes as a web app in Chrome OS. When signed in, you can create playlists of favorite videos to watch later.

- **YouTube Music**. Formerly known as Google Play Music, this music-streaming service offers a vast catalog of tracks. If you don't want adverts, you can pay for a monthly subscription.

- **Chrome Web Store**. This is the place to visit to browse and search for more web apps, games, themes, and extensions to add extra features and functionality to your Chromebook.

- **Play Store**. Modern Chromebooks can run Android apps, and this is where to find and install them. Browse thousands of apps and games; many are free to install, but may offer in-app purchases.

- **Settings**. This app enables you to access all the settings for your Chromebook. You can manage accounts, connected devices, security and privacy, and personalize the look of your desktop.

Hot tip

If you prefer Spotify for streaming music, you can install the Spotify web app.

14

Navigating the desktop

The desktop itself is similar to Windows or macOS. App or browser windows can be resized by dragging the edges or corners; the icons at their top right are used to minimize the window, maximize it (fill the screen), or close it. We'll take a more detailed look at the Chrome OS desktop interface in Chapter 3.

2 Getting Up and Running

So, you've just got your new Chromebook and want to start using it? In this chapter, we show you how to get it up and running. While you can use a guest account, you'll need to sign in with a Google account to get the most out of it.

If your Chromebook doesn't double up as a tablet, don't try pushing the screen back too far.

A tour of the Chromebook

Let's take a look around a typical Chromebook – its input and output ports, keyboard, and display. Note that there is a wide range of Chromebook models, each of which may have different ports, located in different places. The keyboard layout may also vary slightly. However, the main form factor should be fairly similar. There will be a port for the mains power lead, a keyboard, and a screen (which, on a modern Chromebook, may well be touch-sensitive so that you can tap and swipe on it).

Here, we are taking a look at the Acer Spin 311 Chromebook, a fairly typical "2-in-1" model that doubles up as a touchscreen tablet when you fold the screen right back.

Power port
Your Chromebook will have a power port to plug in the mains adaptor supplied with it. This may be of a standard connector type, such as USB-C (see page 174), but it's advisable to stick to the computer's own power supply rather than using a different one.

The first time you unpack your Chromebook, you'll probably need to plug it into the mains to charge up its battery. You should be able to start it up while charging, however, by pressing the **Power** button. On our Acer Spin 311, this is located on the side of the Chromebook, next to the power port.

USB ports
Your Chromebook will have one or more USB ports for connecting peripherals (such as a mouse or external keyboard), storage devices (such as a USB stick drive), and an external monitor. USB ports come in two main types:

- **USB-A.** The original USB style, this is still the most common type and is recognizable from its flat rectangular shape.
- **USB-C.** This more modern USB connector type is smaller with rounded edges. It can carry more power, so may also be used for

a power port. Unlike USB-A, it is also reversible, so it doesn't matter which way round you insert the cable.

Keyboard and touchpad

To enter text, you'll use the Chromebook's built-in keyboard. While this has a similar layout to keyboards on other laptops, there are some notable differences. One thing you may notice is the lack of a **Caps Lock** key. Instead, there's an **Everything Button** (🔍 or ⊙, depending on your Chromebook model). This is used for many purposes, including searching for apps and files.

The touchpad below the keyboard is used to move the cursor arrow around the screen, and for swiping gestures. See Chapter 4 for more details on both the keyboard and touchpad.

You can activate and deactivate Caps Lock by pressing **Alt** and the **Everything Button** together.

The keyboard and touchpad settings can be adjusted in the settings. See Chapter 4 for more details.

17

Display

Like any laptop, the Chromebook has a built-in display, although it is possible to also use an external monitor (see Chapter 12). Chromebook screens range in size from 10.1 to 17.3 inches, but always have a 16:9 widescreen aspect ratio. Many are touchscreens that can be tapped and swiped instead of using the touchpad. This is particularly useful when running Android apps.

Connecting to the internet

While a Chromebook can be used offline, it will need to be connected to the internet when you first start it up. This will enable you to sign in with a Google account, set everything up, and access websites, files, and apps online.

Naturally, you will need to make sure that your wireless broadband router is turned on and connected to the internet.

1 Upon starting up the Chromebook, you will be prompted to sign in with an existing Google account or create a new one (see page 20). Either way, you will be asked to connect the Chromebook to the internet.

2 The Chromebook should scan for available wireless networks in the vicinity. Click on yours.

Your wireless router's name (Service Set IDentifier, or SSID) and password can usually be found written on its rear or on a removable card.

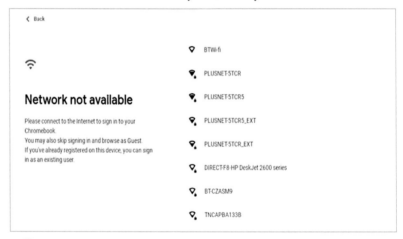

3 You will be asked to enter the password for your wireless router. If you don't know the password, and haven't changed it, you should be able to find it on the back of the router.

Signing in to an account

With the Chromebook
connected to the
internet, you'll be asked
who to add to the
Chromebook: you or a
child. Once you have
selected an option, you
will be asked to sign in
to your Google account.

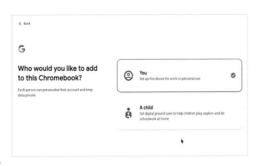

If you already have a Google account set up from another
computer or device, you can sign in to your Chromebook using
that. If not, you can click the **Create account** option, as
covered on page 20.

1 To sign in,
enter the email
address for your
Google account,
which will
usually end in
gmail.com
(unless you
are using a

work email address for a company that has a Google
Workspace account with a custom email domain).

2 Enter the password for your account. Click the **Show
password** box if you want to view it as you type it.

3 You'll be asked to sync your account; click **Accept and
continue**. Next, accept the terms of service for Google
Play. If you like, you can opt in to Google Assistant and
permit it to view your screen, and get it to recognize
your voice by saying a couple of phrases. If you have an
Android phone nearby, you may also be asked if you want
to connect it.

4 Finally, you'll see a screen saying "You're ready!" Click on
the **Get started** button to be taken to the Chrome OS
desktop with a welcome screen.

If activated, Google
Assistant can be
triggered by saying
"OK Google" or "Hey
Google". Then, you can
ask it a question.

If you opt to connect
your Android phone,
you can sign in on the
Chromebook just by
unlocking the phone –
no password required.

Creating a new Google account

If you don't yet have a Google account with which to sign in to the Chromebook, you will need to create one. You can either do this on another computer or device or simply by clicking the **Create account** option on the Sign-in screen.

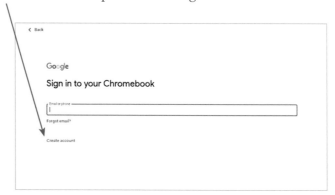

Hot tip

It's best to add a mobile phone number to your account in case you ever forget your password.

1 Enter your first and last name. On the next screen, enter your basic information: birth date and gender.

2 Choose a username for your account, which could be your own name or something else. Click **Next**. If you get a message saying that name

is already taken, you'll need to alter it – maybe by adding some numbers at the end – or select one of the suggested alternatives.

Don't forget

Memorize your Google account password and don't share it with anyone else. Alternatively, you could store it using a password vault service such as LastPass.

3 You'll be prompted to create a strong password. This should comprise a mixture of letters and digits (and possibly symbols) and be long and obscure enough to prevent anyone from guessing it.

4 You have the option of adding a phone number to the account, which is useful if you ever need to retrieve a lost password. On the next screen, review the name and email address and click **Next**.

Using Chromebook as a guest

Instead of signing in with a Google account, it is possible to use the Chromebook as a guest. While this mode has quite a few limitations, it's ideal if you want to let someone else use your Chromebook without gaining access to your Google profile, browser history, bookmarks, and files (including those stored locally on the Chromebook). It can also be useful for troubleshooting if you are having issues signing in.

1 If you are already signed in to a Google account, expand the Status Area panel on the desktop and click the **Sign out** option.

2 On the Lock screen where you are asked to sign in, click the **Browse as Guest** option.

3 You will be taken to the Chrome OS desktop as usual, but there will be only a few core apps available, including the Chrome web browser and Files.

4 To leave Guest mode and return to the Sign-in screen, open up the Status Area panel again and click on **Exit guest**.

Beware

Any files downloaded or bookmarks created during a guest session will be deleted when you exit it. Transfer files to an external storage device to save them.

Hot tip

To expand the Status Area panel, click on the time at the bottom right of the desktop, or press **Alt** + **Shift** + **s**.

Adding extra users

You can add multiple user accounts to your Chromebook so that family members can use it and save their own files, bookmarks, and browsing history. The process is similar to when you added the first account.

Adding a new user

1 If you are already signed in to a Google account, expand the Status Area panel on the desktop and click the **Sign out** option.

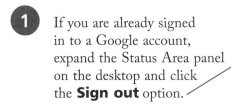

2 On the Lock screen where you are asked to sign in, click on the **Add Person** option.

3 Choose to add an adult (you) or child account and click **Next**. Then, sign in with your username and password for an existing Google account or choose to create a new one (as shown on page 20).

Removing a user

If you later want to remove a user from the Chromebook, sign out of the account you're in. On the Lock screen, click the **Down** arrow to the right of the password field and then click **Remove account**.

You'll see a message warning you that all local files and data will be deleted. If you're sure you want to remove the user, click **Remove account**.

Don't forget

You can't remove the main user account (known as the "owner") that you used to first sign in to the Chromebook.

Beware

Removing an account will delete any files for it stored locally on the Chromebook, so if you need any of them, copy them to your Google Drive or an external storage device first.

3 Navigating the Chrome OS Desktop

The Chrome OS desktop on your Chromebook may look similar to that in other operating systems, but it has some unique features and quirks. This chapter takes you on a tour of the desktop and explores some of its main features.

Around the desktop

Just like any other personal computer, a Chromebook has a main desktop screen from which you can access its applications, files, settings, and other features.

Unlike most desktops, the one in Chrome OS is not littered with icons. So, when you don't have a browser window or application open, you can admire the background "wallpaper" in all its glory.

At the bottom of the desktop is the Shelf, similar to the Taskbar in Windows. Along with any apps currently in use, it shows "pinned" apps and files for quick access. It is also home to the app Launcher and the Status Area.

Let's take a more detailed tour of the desktop and the functionality it offers…

Desktop

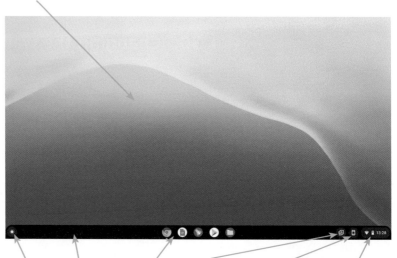

Launcher   Shelf   Pinned apps   Tote   Phone Hub   Status Area

Hot tip

See page 30 for details on how to change your desktop wallpaper.

- **Desktop**. Unlike the desktop in most other operating systems such as Windows and macOS, the Chrome OS desktop always remains blank and is never cluttered with the icons of applications and files. When you first start up your Chromebook, the desktop will feature the default "wallpaper" background image, but this can be switched using the Wallpaper app to any of the numerous wallpapers available or even your own custom image.

- **Shelf**. Similar to the Taskbar in Windows, or the Dock in macOS, this is a useful area where you can access applications and files easily. It is also home to the Launcher (on the left) and Status Area (on the right). While the Shelf is at the bottom of the screen by default, you can move it to another position if you want. You can also opt to autohide the Shelf if you prefer it not to show when using the Chrome browser or other apps, so that you have more room on the screen. We'll take a more detailed look at the Shelf and its options on page 26.

- **Launcher**. Clicking the round icon, or scrolling up the Shelf with a two-finger upward swipe on the touchpad, brings up the Launcher for installed apps and favorite websites. In the Search box, you can search the computer for apps and settings – or search the web for something in the Chrome browser. Scrolling up further, with another two-finger swipe, reveals the apps you have installed on the computer. To close the Launcher, simply click on the Shelf. We'll explore the Launcher in more detail on page 28.

- **Pinned apps**. In the middle of the Shelf are the icons of any currently open apps, or those that have been pinned here for easy access. Just click on an app's icon to open it. Web page shortcuts may also be pinned to the Shelf.

- **Tote**. Sort of like a handy tote bag, this is where you'll find recent and pinned files for easy access. If you don't want it to show file previews in the Shelf, you can right-click it and select **Hide previews**.

- **Phone Hub**. This is where you can connect to an Android smartphone to do things like access its wireless hotspot, locate the device if missing, and view Chrome tabs open on it. We'll explore this option further in Chapter 12.

- **Status Area**. This area shows notifications, Wi-Fi signal, battery level, and the time. Click on the right-hand side to expand the panel for options and settings. We'll explore the Status Area and its options in more detail on page 27.

You can also bring up the Launcher by pressing the **Everything Button** (Q or ⬤, depending on your Chromebook model).

25

You can create additional desktops (called "desks") in **Overview** mode – accessed by pressing the ▢ǁ key on the keyboard – and switch between them (see page 35).

About the Shelf

As mentioned, the Shelf on the Chrome OS desktop is akin to the Taskbar you may be used to using in Windows, or the Dock in macOS, and offers similar functionality. It plays host to the icons of currently open or pinned applications (and websites) in the middle. Just click on an icon to open the relevant app/site, or hover the cursor above it to view its name.

You can pin your favorite apps to the Shelf for easy access.

Shelf position

While the Shelf's default position is at the bottom of the desktop, you can move it to either side of the screen if you prefer. Just right-click (two-finger click/tap on touchpad/screen) on an empty part of the desktop, select **Shelf position**, and choose **Left**, **Bottom**, or **Right**.

Autohiding the Shelf

To free up more space on the screen, there's an option to automatically hide the Shelf when you are using an app or browsing the web. To access this option, right-click on a bare part of the Shelf and select **Autohide shelf.** Once you've activated the autohide setting, you can make the Shelf reappear by moving the cursor to the edge of the screen (the bottom by default) where it normally resides. You can also reset the Shelf to stay visible by right-clicking and selecting **Always show shelf**.

Accessing the Status Area

Located at the right end of the Shelf, the Status Area shows useful information such as the strength of the Wi-Fi signal to your wireless router, the battery charge level, and the current time. Notifications will also appear above this area at times, to inform you of things like apps being updated.

Expanding the Status Area

To expand the Status Area into a full panel, simply left-click on it. (You may also need to click the upward-pointing arrow at the top right.) You will then be able to see its full range of settings and options. Let's take a quick look at them:

- **Sign out**. Click this if you want to sign out of your account completely and return to the Lock screen where you sign in.
- **Shut down**. Click the icon to the right of the **Sign out** option to shut down the computer and turn it **Off**.
- **Lock**. The next icon along will lock the computer while you're away from your desk, requiring a sign-in with your password to continue.
- **Settings**. The cog icon will open up the Chrome OS **Settings** window. We'll explore the options available there in more detail in Chapter 13.
- **Screen capture**. This brings up options for capturing still images or video recordings of your computer screen.
- **Nearby visibility**. Click this to see settings for the **Nearby Share** feature, which can be used to easily transfer files between multiple Chromebooks and Android devices.
- **Night Light**. Turn this **On** to automatically adjust the screen color to a warmer shade at night. You can use the sunrise/sunset times for your location or set custom start/end times.
- **Audio volume**. A slider to adjust the sound volume. Click the arrow to its right to access the audio settings.
- **Brightness**. A slider to adjust the screen brightness.

You can also expand the Status Area quickly by pressing **Alt** + **Shift** + **s**. You'll also see any new notifications above the panel.

Click on the second dot above the audio volume bar, or two-finger swipe right, to see extra options such as **Cast**.

You can also use the keyboard shortcut + **Ctrl** + **Shift** + ⬚ to bring up the screen-capture options.

27

Using the Launcher

The Launcher is the place to find all of your installed apps – both Chrome and Android ones – and also any favorite websites for which you've created a shortcut in Chrome (by clicking the three dots at the top right, selecting **More Tools**, and then **Create shortcut...**).

There are three ways to bring up the Launcher. You can press the **Everything Button** (⬤ or ⬤, depending on your Chromebook model) on the keyboard. Alternatively, click the round icon at the left end of the Shelf or scroll the latter up with a two-finger swipe up.

Search tool

In the Search box at the top of the Launcher, you can search your Chromebook for installed apps and settings by name. You can even search the web for something here, with results appearing in the Chrome browser.

All apps

Use a two-finger swipe up gesture to scroll the Launcher up further to see the first "page" of apps in a grid format. To move between pages of apps in the Launcher, use two-finger down or up swipes from above the Shelf, or click one of the dots to the right of the app grid to select a page.

Hot tip

The default for scrolling down between Launcher pages (and in the Chrome browser) is to swipe down, but this can be changed – in **Settings**, go to **Device** > **Touchpad** > **Enable reverse scrolling**.

Managing apps

To launch an app from the Launcher grid, or a pinned app on the Shelf, simply click on its icon.

Arranging apps

By default, Chrome OS will arrange your apps automatically in the Launcher grid, with the pre-installed ones on the first page, and any newly installed Android apps together on a later page. However, it's possible to rearrange them. To do so, click and hold the app icon, then drag it to a new position in the grid. It's also possible to move it between pages by dragging it to the top or bottom.

Don't forget

When you move apps into a folder, their individual icons will disappear from the main Launcher page and will only be found within the folder.

Other app icons will shuffle around automatically to make room. If you drop your app icon onto another one, however, you can create a folder and name it. This is a useful way of organizing apps with a similar purpose (e.g. music apps).

Pinning an app

If you have a favorite app that you use a lot, you may want to pin it to the Shelf for easier access. To do so, right-click it in the Launcher grid, then select **Pin to shelf**. To unpin it again, right-click it on the Shelf or in the Launcher and select **Unpin from shelf**.

Uninstalling an app

If there's an app you no longer need, right-click on it in the Launcher grid and select **Uninstall**. Note that some core apps such as Chrome and Files cannot be uninstalled.

Hot tip

To remove an app from a folder, simply drag it out and drop it into a space on the main Launcher page.

Changing the wallpaper

The default wallpaper for the desktop looks fine, but you may well want to change it to another image to personalize your Chromebook experience. Here's how to do it.

1 Right-click on the desktop and select the **Set wallpaper** option. This will open up the Wallpaper Picker app.

Beware

If you switch from the default wallpaper and then want it back, it's not available in the menu, so you'll need to download an image of it.

2 Choose one of the image categories on the left-hand side of the window, such as Cityscapes. Scroll down the main

area of the window to see a wide selection of wallpapers. Simply click on one to use it: your desktop will switch instantly to show it.

3 Selecting the top-left image, marked **Daily Refresh**, will lead to it changing automatically on a daily basis, so your desktop will look different each day.

4 The categories on the left also include a **My Images** option. Select this to use an image stored locally on

your Chromebook – if you want to use a photo from your Google Photos library or Google Drive, etc., you'll need to download it first. Scrolling back up to the top, you'll find options for **Center** and **Center Cropped** – the latter scales the image to fit the screen.

4 Keyboard and Touchpad

As on any other laptop, the keyboard is used to enter text, while the touchpad is used to navigate and interact with on-screen items. In this chapter, we explore both input devices and some of their unique features on the Chromebook.

Around the keyboard

Chromebooks have the same data input devices as most laptops: a keyboard to input text, and a touchpad to navigate. However, the keyboard has a few noticeable differences, such as a different key in place of **Caps Lock** on the left, and – instead of numbered function keys – unique "Chromebook" keys running along the top.

The touchpad below the keyboard enables a number of special gestures using single or multiple finger swipes and taps.

The Everything Button
Found on the left of the keyboard, between **Tab** and **Shift**, the **Everything Button** will have a ⌕ or ◉ symbol on it, depending on your model of Chromebook.

As the name implies, it is a multipurpose key. Tapping it on its own will open up the Launcher Search bar from the Shelf on the desktop. Tap the key again to close it.

Pressing the **Shift** key with the **Everything Button** brings up the Launcher app grid to show all the applications you have installed.

The **Everything Button** can also be combined with other keys for other functions such as selecting sections of text in a document, locking the screen, and opening the Clipboard menu. We detail the most useful keyboard shortcuts on pages 34-37.

Chromebook keys
The top row of the keyboard comprises mainly special Chromebook keys with symbols on them. Depending on your model of Chromebook, you may have a smaller selection of them.

← Go to the previous page

→ Go to the next page

C Refresh the current page

⛶ Make your page take up the full screen

⧉ Show all your open windows (**Overview** mode)

☼ Decrease screen brightness

☼ Increase screen brightness

🔇 Mute the sound

🔉 Decrease sound volume

🔊 Increase sound volume

⧉ Take a screenshot

▨ Turn on electronic privacy screen

⚊ Decrease keyboard backlight brightness

⚌ Increase keyboard backlight brightness

Hot tip

These Chromebook keys can also work as standard function keys – see page 40.

Useful keyboard shortcuts

As on most other computers, you can use keyboard shortcuts to quickly access a range of functions. These require a certain combination of keys pressed together at the same time. For instance, "**Ctrl** + **Tab**" means pressing the **Ctrl** and **Tab** keys together. There are a whole lot of shortcuts in Chrome OS, which you can view by pressing **Ctrl** + **Alt** + **/**. Here, we'll cover some of the most useful ones.

Tabs and windows

Ctrl + **Tab**	Go to next tab
Shift + **Ctrl** + **Tab**	Go to previous tab
Ctrl + **1** to **8**	Go to tabs one to eight
Ctrl + **9**	Go to last tab
Ctrl + **l** or **Alt** + **d**	Focus on address bar
Ctrl + **t**	Open a new tab
Ctrl + **n**	Open a new window
Ctrl + **Shift** + **n**	Open a new window in **Incognito** mode
Ctrl + **w**	Close the current tab
Ctrl + **Shift** + **w**	Close the current window
Ctrl + **Shift** + **t**	Reopen the last tab or window you closed
Ctrl + **Shift** + **a**	Search tabs

Alt + **=**   Maximize window (or revert)

Alt + **-**   Minimize window

Hold **Alt**, press **Tab**   Switch quickly between windows

Ctrl + **Shift** and   Open the link in a new tab and switch to
click a link   the new tab

Shift and click a link Open the link in a new window

Ctrl + **o**   Open a file in the browser

Desktop
(🔍 or ⦿) + **[**   Activate the desk on the left

(🔍 or ⦿) + **]**   Activate the desk on the right

Shift + (🔍 or ⦿) + **=**   Create a new desk

Shift + (🔍 or ⦿) + **[**   Move active windows to the desk on
                                the left

Shift + (🔍 or ⦿) + **]**   Move active windows to the desk on
                                the right

Alt + (🔍 or ⦿) + **m**   Move active window between displays

Text
Ctrl + **c**   Copy selected text

Ctrl + **x**   Cut selected text

Ctrl + **v**   Paste selected text

You can see all your windows and desks in **Overview** mode – accessed by pressing the ▭|| key.

You can connect the Chromebook to an external display – see Chapter 12 for more details.

...cont'd

(⌕ or ◉) + **v**	Open Clipboard
Alt + (⌕ or ◉)	Turn **Caps Lock On** and **Off**
(⌕ or ◉) + ◀	Go to beginning of line
(⌕ or ◉) + ▶	Go to end of line
Ctrl + (⌕ or ◉) + ◀	Go to beginning of document
Ctrl + (⌕ or ◉) + ▶	Go to end of document
Ctrl + ▶	Move to end of next word
Ctrl + ◀	Move to start of previous word
Ctrl + **a**	Select everything on the page
Ctrl + **z**	Undo your last action
Ctrl + **Shift** + **z**	Redo your last action

Screenshots and recording

Ctrl + ⊡	Take full-screen screenshot
Shift + **Ctrl** + ⊡	Take partial screenshot
Ctrl + **Alt** + ⊡	Take window screenshot/recording

Docking windows

Alt + [	Dock a window on the left
Alt +]	Dock a window on the right

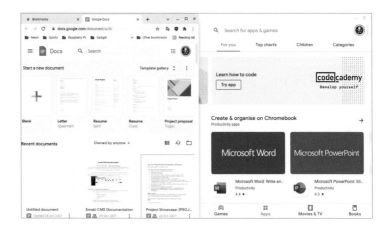

...cont'd

Pages and web browser

Alt + ▶	Go forward to next page
Alt + ◀	Go back to previous page
(🔍 or ⊙) + ▶	Go to bottom of page
(🔍 or ⊙) + ◀	Go to top of page
Ctrl + **Shift** + **b**	Show the Bookmarks bar
Alt + **Shift** + **b**	Focus on or highlight the Bookmarks bar
Ctrl + **=**	Zoom in on page
Ctrl + **-**	Zoom out of page
Ctrl + **0**	Reset zoom level on page
Ctrl + **d**	Save current tab as a bookmark
Ctrl + **f**	Search current page
Ctrl + **Shift** + **o**	Show Bookmark Manager

Other useful shortcuts

(🔍 or ⊙) + **l**	Lock screen
(🔍 or ⊙) + **a**	Open Google Assistant

Alt + **Shift** + **m**	Open the Files app
Alt + **Shift** + **s**	Open the Status Area
Shift + (🔍 or ⊙)	Open the full-screen Launcher
Ctrl + **Alt** + **t**	Open Crosh window

Hot tip

Akin to the Command Prompt on Windows or Terminal in macOS devices, Crosh allows users to run commands in Chrome OS.

To open the Settings app, either find it in the Launcher or open the Status Area at the bottom right and click the **Settings** icon.

You can quickly change back to the last used keyboard input method by pressing **Ctrl** + **Space**. Or, press **Ctrl** + **Shift** + **Space** to cycle forward through your added input methods.

You can find your added keyboard methods, and switch between them, by opening the **Status Area** and clicking the **Keyboard** option (on the second page of options).

Special characters

When typing a text document, sometimes you will want to add a letter with an accent, or a special symbol. Let's take a look at how to enter these special characters.

Enabling international keyboard

The easiest way to access letters with accents is to switch to the US international keyboard input (if you are not already using it).

1 Open the Settings app and, in the left panel, select **Advanced** and then **Languages and inputs**. In the main panel, click on **Inputs**, then **+ Add input methods**.

2 From the list, select the option **English (US) with International keyboard**. Then, click **Add**.

3 In **Input Methods**, click on **English (US) with International keyboard**. It will say **Enabled** under it.

Typing accented characters

With the US international keyboard enabled, you can access some shortcuts to type accented characters.

Acute (´)	', then letter
Grave (`)	`, then letter
Tilde (~)	**Shift** + ` then letter

Circumflex (^)	**Shift** + **6** then letter
Umlaut/diaeresis (¨)	**Shift** + **'** then letter
Cedilla (¸)	**Shift** + **AltGr** + **5** then letter
Acute (é)	**AltGr** + **e**
Acute (á)	**AltGr** + **a**
Acute (ú)	**AltGr** + **u**
Acute (í)	**AltGr** + **i**
Acute (ó)	**AltGr** + **o**
Tilde (ñ)	**AltGr** + **n**
Umlaut/diaeresis (ü)	**AltGr** + **y**
Umlaut/diaeresis (ö)	**AltGr** + **p**
Umlaut/diaeresis (ä)	**AltGr** + **q**
Cedilla (ç)	**AltGr** + **,**

Typing symbols

In Google Workspace office applications such as Docs (see Chapter 8), you can find symbols and other special characters by choosing **Insert**, then **Special characters**.

Alternatively, you can enter special characters using their Unicode number. Press **Ctrl** + **Shift** + **u**, then the code. For instance, to type the © copyright symbol, the code is 00A9. After entering it, press

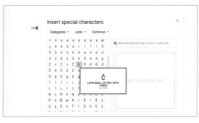

Space and the symbol will appear. You can even enter emojis this way, such as grinning face – 1F600. For a full list of Unicode characters, visit **home.unicode.org**

Hot tip

You will also find a large number of international characters in the **Insert** > **Special characters** menu.

Caps Lock and function keys

Turning on Caps Lock

One of the most noticeable differences on a Chromebook keyboard is the absence of a **Caps Lock** key.

1 To turn **Caps Lock On**, press the **Alt** key and **Everything Button** (Q or ◉) together.

2 To turn **Caps Lock Off**, simply press the **Alt** key and **Everything Button** together again.

Using function keys

Another noticeable feature of the Chromebook keyboard is the lack of the usual numbered function keys (F1, F2, etc.) in the top row. These are replaced with Chromebook keys marked with symbols for special functions (see page 33).

If you do need to access function keys, press the **Everything Button** along with one of the Chromebook keys. Starting with ← for F1, they are numbered from left to right.

Alternatively, to make all the Chromebook keys behave as function keys by default, do the following:

1 Open the **Settings** app and select **Device** in the left-hand panel, then **Keyboard** in the main panel.

2 Now, click the **Treat top-row keys as function keys** option.

3 With this option activated, you can still use the keys' Chromebook functions by pressing them with the **Everything Button**.

Hot tip

You can use the **Keyboard** settings to alter how keys such as **Ctrl** and **Alt** function.

Using the touchpad

As on any other laptop computer, your Chromebook features a touchpad below the keyboard. This is used in place of a mouse to move the pointer arrow on screen and select items.

- **Navigation**. Swipe a single finger around the touchpad to move the on-screen pointer. If you reach the edge of the touchpad and want to continue moving the pointer in that direction, just lift your finger up and swipe again.
- **Click**. To click (i.e. left-click) on something under the pointer, either tap the touchpad or click it down in its lower half.
- **Right-click**. To right-click on something, tap the touchpad with two fingers at the same time or click it down with two fingers in its lower half. Alternatively, you can press the **Alt** key with a single-finger tap/click.

There are numerous other touchpad gestures, which we'll explore on page 42.

Touchpad settings

You can change how the touchpad functions. Open the **Settings** app, select the **Device** option in the left panel, then select **Touchpad**. The options are as follows:

- **Enable tap-to-click**. Turned **On** by default, this enables you to tap the touchpad lightly to perform a click.
- **Enable tap dragging**. This allows you to drag an item with one finger, by double-tapping it (quickly), then holding your finger and swiping.
- **Enable touchpad acceleration**. Enabled by default, this means the distance traveled by the on-screen pointer depends on the speed of your touchpad swipe.
- **Touchpad speed**. Adjust how quickly the pointer moves when you swipe on the touchpad.
- **Enable reverse scrolling**. Reverse the direction of scrolling when you do a two-finger swipe up or down.

If the touchpad isn't working as expected, check the **Touchpad** settings to see if you've changed them.

Touchpad gestures

Here are some of the gestures you can use on the touchpad to access various functions:

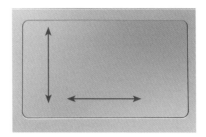

- **Move pointer**. Move your finger across the touchpad.
- **Click**. Tap the touchpad or press its lower half.
- **Right-click**. Tap or press the touchpad with two fingers. Or, press the **Alt** key and click with one finger.
- **Scroll**. Place two fingers on the touchpad and move them up and down to scroll vertically, or left and right to scroll horizontally in a wide document.
- **Move between pages**. To go back to a page you were just on, swipe left with two fingers. To go forward to a page you were just on, swipe right with two fingers.
- **Close a tab**. Point to the tab, then tap or click the touchpad with three fingers.
- **Open a link in a new tab**. Point to the link, then tap or click the touchpad with three fingers.
- **Switch between tabs**. If you have multiple browser tabs open, swipe left or right with three fingers.
- **Open or close Overview mode**. To open **Overview** mode showing all open windows and desks, swipe up with three fingers. To close it, swipe down with three fingers.
- **Switch between virtual desks**. If you have multiple desks open, swipe left or right with four fingers.
- **Drag and drop**. Using one finger, click and hold the item that you want to move. Drag the item to its new spot, then release your finger.

Don't forget

You can add virtual desks in **Overview** mode or with the keyboard shortcut shown on page 35.

5 Using the Chrome Browser

As well as being the world's most popular web browser, Chrome is a key part of the Chrome OS operating system and is used as the basis for many apps. Find out how to make the most of Chrome's features in this chapter.

Don't forget

An exception is Android apps, which run in their own windows and not inside Chrome. Find out more about them and other apps in Chapter 10.

44

Tour of the browser

One of the most important parts of Chrome OS is the Chrome web browser. As it's the world's most popular web browser, you may well have used it on another computer, tablet, or smartphone, and it functions in much the same way on your Chromebook.

However, not only does Chrome enable you to visit websites, but many of the applications that you use on your Chromebook will be run in a Chrome window.

Before we go into the details of Chrome's features and how to make the most of them, let's take a tour of the Chrome web browser:

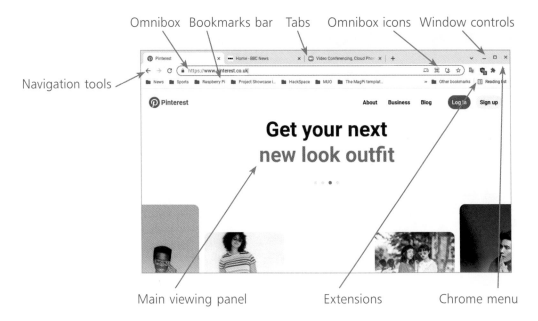

Omnibox Bookmarks bar Tabs Omnibox icons Window controls

Navigation tools

Main viewing panel   Extensions   Chrome menu

- **Omnibox**. Also known as the address bar, this is where you can enter either a web address or a search term. It has some powerful and helpful features that we'll explore later in this chapter.
- **Tabs**. Instead of opening a new window to visit a new web page while keeping another site open, it's easier to load multiple web pages in separate tabs. Simply click the **+** symbol to the right of the last tab to create a new one. You can switch between tabs easily by clicking on one. They can be rearranged

by clicking and dragging them left and right. They can also be grouped together so that they can be moved as one, collapsed into one tab when not in use (to save space), or opened in a new window.

- **Main viewing panel**. This is where you view web pages and click on the links found within them. By default, a new tab or window will take you to **google.com** with a Search bar and your most visited sites below it, but this can be altered in the Chrome settings. Use two-finger swipes up and down on the touchpad to scroll the page up and down.

- **Bookmarks bar**. Displayed under the Omnibox, this bar shows any websites, or folders containing several websites, that you have bookmarked and added to the **Bookmarks bar** folder (or a sub-folder created within it in the Bookmark Manager). By default, the Bookmarks bar is hidden – to show it (or hide it again), press **Ctrl** + **Shift** + **b**.

- **Navigation tools**. You can click these icons to navigate back and forth between previously loaded pages and refresh the current page.

- **Omnibox icons**. Clicking the ☆ icon here enables you to add a bookmark for the current page. Other icons that may appear here at certain times enable you to manage saved passwords, install or open an app for certain websites, send the current web page to another device on which you are signed in, and create a QR code for the page.

- **Extensions**. This is where you will find any extensions you have installed from the Chrome Web Store.

- **Chrome menu**. Click the ⋮ icon to open a menu with numerous options including History, Downloads, Bookmarks, Zoom, Print, Cast, and Settings.

- **Window controls**. Minimize, maximize, or close a window.

A QR (Quick Response) code is a two-dimensional barcode that can be scanned by a camera and processed to reveal its information such as a web address.

Extensions add extra functionality to the Chrome web browser. For details on how to install them, see page 151.

The Omnibox

Found near the top of the Chrome window, the Omnibox offers the quickest and easiest way to start your journey surfing the World Wide Web. By typing in the Omnibox, you can search for terms online or enter a website address to go to it directly.

Omnibox history

Some people may refer to the Omnibox as the "address bar". Indeed, this is the standard term for it in other web browsers such as Microsoft Edge and Mozilla Firefox. This name stuck because early web browsers would only use the bar at the top of the window to input web addresses – to search for something, the user would first need to visit a search-engine website such as **google.com** or **yahoo.com**

Google thought it would make things a whole lot more convenient by combining both search and web address input functions in the one bar, and thus the Omnibox was born, launched back in 2008 with the very first version of Chrome. Other web browsers soon followed suit by combining both functions in the address bar.

Entering a search term

To search for anything on the World Wide Web in Chrome, simply type the search term – e.g. "presidents of the USA" – into the Omnibox and press the **Enter** key (↵).

To add **www.** and **.com** to your search term to turn it into a web address, press **Ctrl** + **Enter**.

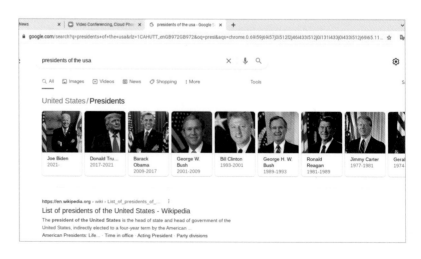

The web page panel below should update quickly to show the results of your search using the Google search engine (by default, although this can be changed – see page 68 for more details). Scroll down the page to see further results. At the bottom of the page, you can click on **Next** for the next page of results, or click one of the page numbers.

Just above the page numbers, you may see a group of **Related searches** that Google thinks you may be interested in, especially if the original search didn't give you the results you were after. If so, simply click on one of these items to perform a new search with that term.

Related searches ⋮

Q presidents **in order**

Q who is the **46th president**

Q **list** of presidents **and years**

Q **printable list** of presidents in order

Q **which** presidents **were democrats and republicans**

Q **first president** of usa

Q **who is** the **president** of the united states 2021

Q **vice president** of usa

Goooooooooogle ›

1 2 3 4 5 6 7 8 9 10   Next

Automatic suggestions

As you type a search term into the Omnibox, you may notice that Chrome will come up with a list of suggestions below the Omnibox for what it thinks you may be looking for. These may include sites you've already visited and terms you've searched for previously. To select one, simply click on it to search for that term.

Hot tip

Want to remove a suggestion from the list to stop it reappearing? Hover the mouse cursor over it and click the **X** symbol that appears to its right.

...cont'd

Chrome may also attempt to autocomplete the search term or URL in the Omnibox itself as you type. If you don't want the suggested text appended to what you've typed, press **Ctrl** + **z** to delete it.

While this autocompletion feature may prove useful, some users may find it a little annoying. Fortunately, it can be turned off in Chrome's settings. Click the ⋮ icon at the top left, select **Settings**, then **Sync and Google Services**. Now, click the blue switch next to **Autocomplete searches and URLs** to turn the feature **Off**.

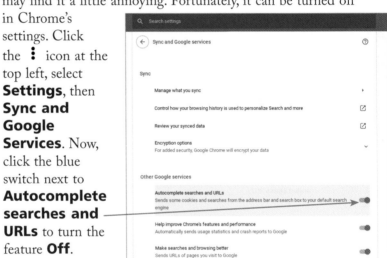

Omnibox icons

As mentioned during our tour of the browser at the start of this chapter, the right-hand end of the Omnibox may also show a range of different icons. Note that some of these only appear when you visit a certain website, such as one with an installable app, or when you click in the Omnibox. Let's take a closer look at some of the icons that appear here:

- ☆ Click the star icon to bookmark the current web page or add it to your reading list so that you can easily return to it later. To find out more about using bookmarks, see pages 53-55; for more details on the reading list, see page 56.

- ⤓ This icon only appears on certain websites, such as Pinterest, and enables you to install an app for that site.

- ⬀ If you already have an app installed for a site, this icon will appear in the Omnibox. Click it to open the relevant app.

Don't forget

If you install an app, its icon will appear in the Launcher grid. You can also pin it to the Shelf for quick access.

...cont'd

- ⬚ Click this to send the current web page to another device on which you are signed in to Chrome with the same account.

- ⬚ Clicking this creates a QR code for the site, which you can download and share so that others can scan it with a phone.

- ⚿ This shows that a username and password have been saved for the current site. Click it to manage your passwords.

Box of tricks

The Omnibox has a number of cool features up its sleeve. Here are just a few:

- Type a calculation (e.g. **37.3 x 293.4**) into it and it will take you to the answer in a calculator.

- Enter a formula, such as **x^2** (x squared), and it will show you a graph for it.

- To open a new document in Google Docs, Sheets, or Slides, type **doc.new**, **sheet.new** or **slide.new**.

- If you want to translate a word or phrase to another language, type it after the word **translate**; e.g. **translate bread to French**. The result will appear and you can use the drop-down menus to change the language to translate to or from.

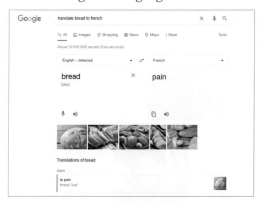

- To set a timer, type **timer** followed by the desired duration – e.g. **timer 30 minutes**. A timer will appear and count down; when it reaches zero, it will start beeping to alert you.

Don't forget

You can also add web page shortcuts to the Launcher grid. To add one from Chrome, click the ⋮ icon at the top right, then select **More tools** > **Create shortcut**.

49

Hot tip

Want to decide something with the flip of a coin or the roll of a dice? Type **flip coin** or **roll dice** – you can even choose how many sides the dice has.

Working with tabs

The ability to add new tabs in the Chrome web browser makes it a lot easier to switch between different web pages without having to open a new window for each one. Simply click a tab to show its current web page.

Adding and closing tabs

To add a new tab, simply click the **+** symbol to the right of the last open tab, or press the **Ctrl** + **t** keyboard shortcut.

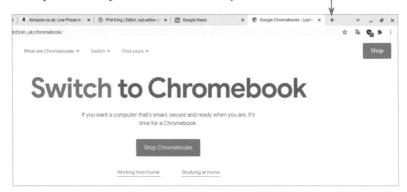

To close a tab, click the **X** symbol to the right of its name, or press **Ctrl** + **w**.

To reopen the last tab (or window) that you closed, use the **Ctrl** + **Shift** + **t** keyboard shortcut.

Viewing and searching all tabs

If you like to use a lot of windows and tabs, it can be hard to keep tabs (no pun intended) on them all. Fortunately, Chrome has a handy tab manager that allows you to browse a list of tabs and even search for the one you're after.

Just click the **Down** arrow icon in Chrome's top bar – just to the left of the window controls (minimize, maximize, and close). Alternatively, press **Ctrl** + **Shift** + **a**.

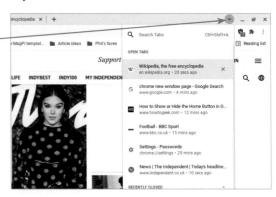

Hot tip

To change the order of tabs, simply drag them left and right.

Don't forget

You can switch between tabs by swiping left or right with three fingers on the touchpad.

Hot tip

You can restore a whole window of tabs by clicking the **⋮** icon, hovering over **History**, then the multiple tabs entry in the list, and selecting **Restore window**.

This will reveal a list not just of the tabs you have open (in any window), but also a list of recently closed tabs. Just click on one to go straight to it (or reopen it) in the browser.

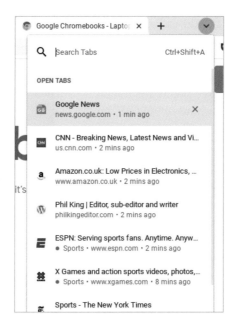

If you want to close a tab listed here, hover the mouse cursor over it in the list and click the **X** symbol that appears next to it.

At the top of the list is a **Search Tabs** box where you can type a search term to look for a particular tab.

Grouping tabs

Another really helpful feature in Chrome is the ability to place tabs together in color-coded groups to help you stay organized. For instance, you might want to group tabs related to a certain topic; e.g. sports.

To create a new group, right-click on a tab and select **Add tab to new group**. Now, choose a color for the group and give it an optional name – if you don't choose one, it will instead be shown as a colored circle in the tabs bar.

You can create multiple groups. If you don't name them, remember to use a different color for each one so that they are easy to spot.

...cont'd

To add an existing tab to a group, simply drag it into a group while the group is expanded – see below for details on how to collapse and expand groups.

To remove a tab from a group, drag it off to the left or right until the tab is no longer outlined with the group's color. Alternatively, right-click on the tab and select **Remove from group**.

Hot tip

You need to have at least one tab open, so you won't be able to collapse all groups if you have no other tabs open.

To save space in the tabs bar, each group can be "collapsed" so that only its name (or colored circle) is shown in the bar; click on the name/circle to expand it again and see all of its tabs.

To see group options, right-click on the group's name (or colored circle). Options include adding a new tab to the group, ungrouping tabs, closing the group, and moving the group to a new window.

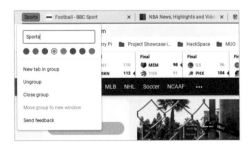

Using bookmarks

When you are browsing the World Wide Web, no doubt you will want to return to your favorite websites or other web pages of interest. Rather than leaving all of their tabs open, you can "bookmark" web pages so that you can easily reopen them later.

Adding a bookmark

To save a bookmark for the currently open web page, follow these steps:

1 Click on the ☆ icon at the far right of the Omnibox.

2 A small menu will appear with the options **Add bookmark** and **Add to reading list**. Click on **Add bookmark**.

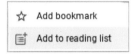

☆ Add bookmark

▤ Add to reading list

To show or hide the Bookmarks bar, press **Ctrl** + **Shift** + **b**.

3 Change the bookmark name in the **Name** field if you like, then select a folder to store it in from the **Folder** drop-down menu. If you can't see a folder you want to use, select **Choose another folder** at the bottom.

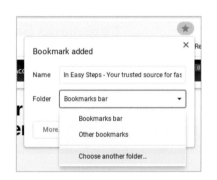

Bookmark added   ✕   Re

Name   In Easy Steps - Your trusted source for fas

Folder   Bookmarks bar ▾

     Bookmarks bar
More...   Other bookmarks

     Choose another folder...

4 If you chose the latter option, a new panel will appear with a view of all of your existing folders (if you have already created some with your Google account in Chrome, possibly on another computer or device). Some of the folders may contain sub-

Edit bookmark

Name   In Easy Steps - Your trusted source for fast learning

URL   https://ineasysteps.com

📁 Bookmarks bar
📁 Other bookmarks

New folder   Cancel   Save

folders; click the arrow next to the folder to reveal them.

...cont'd

Alternatively, you can save the bookmark straight into the main **Bookmarks bar** folder (or create a new folder – see the next page).

5 Click on a folder to select it, then click the **Save** button to save the bookmark there.

Hot tip

You can also store bookmarks in the **Other bookmarks** folder, which will appear at the right side of the Bookmarks bar once it has one or more bookmarks in it.

6 If your bookmark was saved in a folder within the main **Bookmarks bar** folder, you should now be able to find it in the relevant folder in the Bookmarks bar underneath the Omnibox – or on its own if saved directly into the main **Bookmarks bar** folder.

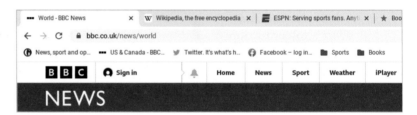

Removing a bookmark

To quickly remove a bookmark for the current web page, click the ☆ icon at the far right of the Omnibox, select **Edit bookmark**, and click the **Remove** button.

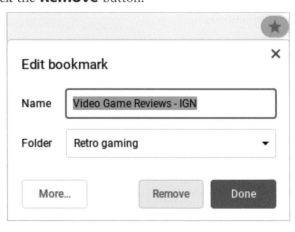

Bookmarks bar

Storing a bookmark directly in the **Bookmarks bar** folder, rather than a sub-folder, will result in it appearing in the Bookmarks bar, shown just below the Omnibox.

If the bar isn't visible, press the **Ctrl** + **Shift** + **b** keyboard shortcut to reveal it.

While the Bookmarks bar is an ideal place to store your most important bookmarks for easy access, it can soon fill up. So, it's best to create sub-folders within it for various topics and store relevant bookmarks within them.

Creating a new folder

When adding a bookmark, you can create a new folder for it by clicking **More...** and then **New folder**. This will create a folder within the currently selected folder – you can even create sub-folders within sub-folders. Type a name for the folder, then click on **Save**.

Bookmark Manager

To help organize your bookmarks, open up the Bookmark Manager with the **Ctrl** + **Shift** + **o** keyboard shortcut. Here, you can rearrange bookmarks and folders by dragging and dropping them. To edit or delete a bookmark, click the ⋮ icon to its right.

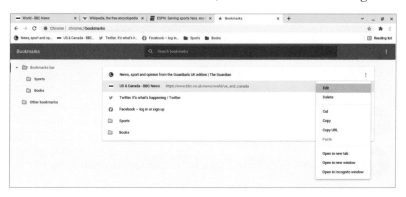

Reading list

Sometimes you may find an interesting article or news story online, but don't have time to read it right now. You might not necessarily want to save it as a bookmark, though. That's where Chrome's reading list features comes in handy: as its name suggests, it's a list of things to read. So, you can save articles, news stories, and other web pages to it and read them later.

Adding a page to the reading list

To save the currently open web page to your reading list, follow these steps:

To help you remember what you've already read, the reading list is divided into two sections: Unread and Pages you've read.

1 Click on the ☆ icon at the far right of the Omnibox.

2 A small menu will appear with the options **Add bookmark** and **Add to reading list**. Click on **Add to reading list**.

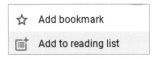

3 The **Reading list** button to the right of the Bookmarks bar will turn blue briefly to show the web page has been added. Click on the button and you'll see the web page at the top, along with any others you've added to the reading list.

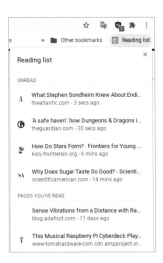

With the reading list open, you can click the X icon to the right of an article to delete it from the list. You can also click the check mark symbol next to an article to mark it as read or unread.

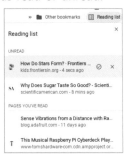

Reading an article from the list

To read a saved article from the reading list:

1 Click the **Reading list** button to open up the list.

2 Click on the desired article in the list to open it in a new tab.

Managing browsing history

Unless you are using **Incognito** mode (find out more about that on page 59), by default Chrome will automatically save the names and URLs of any web pages you visit to your history. You can then view a menu of recently visited pages, or open up the full History page where you can search for pages and delete items from your history.

Viewing the History list

To view a list of recently visited pages, simply press the ⋮ icon and hover the mouse pointer over the **History** option.

The list may include folders of tabs from windows you've closed. Hover over one to see the pages. You can click a page to open it or select **Restore window** to open them all.

Depending on your Google account settings, the History list may also include web pages you've visited on other devices.

Opening the History page

In order to view the detailed History page, either select the bar marked **History** at the top of the recently visited pages list or press the **Ctrl + h** keyboard shortcut at any time.

On the History page, you will see a chronologically ordered list of web pages you've visited. You can search for a particular page by entering a term in the **Search history** box at the top.

...cont'd

You may also see an option in the left panel to view **Tabs from other devices** on which you are signed in with your Google account.

Removing items from History

To remove an item from your history, click the **⋮** icon to its right and select **Remove from history**. Selecting **More from this site** will list other pages from the same website, which may prove useful if you want to delete similar pages.

Alternatively, to delete multiple items quickly and easily, check the boxes to their left and then click the **Delete** button at the top right.

Clearing browsing data

Also found on the left of the History page is an option to **Clear browsing data**. Clicking this opens up a new tab with the relevant **Settings** dialog box open. Here, you can opt to clear your entire browsing history for the time range selected in the drop-down menu. If so, click the box for **Browsing history** and then click **Clear data**.

By checking the other boxes, you can also opt to delete **Cookies and other site data** and/or **Cached images and files**.

The **Advanced** tab offers additional options such as **Download history**.

Beware

Clearing your browsing history for all time may make it difficult to find earlier pages you've visited.

Beware

Clearing cookies will sign you out of websites, so make sure you know how to log in to them again – you can do so more easily if you've saved their passwords in Chrome (see page 62).

Incognito mode

If you want to browse privately, Chrome's **Incognito** mode is a good option. In this mode, none of your browsing history, cookies and site data, or information entered in forms is saved on your device or in Chrome. Therefore, your activity will not show up in your Chrome browser history. So it could be useful, for instance, if you want to browse for gifts for someone who may borrow your device and use Chrome while signed in to your Google account.

Entering Incognito mode

To enjoy private browsing in **Incognito** mode, click the **⋮** icon at the top right of Chrome to open up its menu. Then, click on the **New Incognito window** option there. Alternatively, press the **Ctrl** + **Shift** + **n** keyboard shortcut at any time in Chrome.

Either method will open up a new **Incognito** window with a black background and message saying "You've gone Incognito".

You will still have access to your bookmarks and reading list in **Incognito** mode and be able to save items to them.

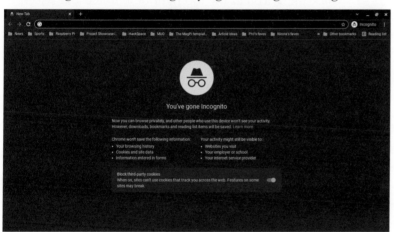

Incognito browsing

While you can browse websites as normal in **Incognito** mode, Chrome will not save the following information:

- Your browsing history

- Cookies and site data

- Information entered in forms

However, note that your activity might still be visible to websites you visit, your employer or school (if using a shared device), and your internet service provider (ISP).

Blocking third-party cookies may cause features on some websites to not work correctly.

Making use of Autofill

Does anyone find filling in forms fun? If can be laborious, repetitive, time-consuming, and plain annoying when you need to keep filling in the same details – such as your name, address, and phone number – on multiple websites when creating a new account or entering delivery information, for instance.

Fortunately, Chrome has a neat trick up its sleeve to save you a whole lot of time and annoyance: **Autofill**.

As the name implies, it can fill in details on web forms automatically for you. Along with contact details, it can also save payment card details and website passwords.

Adding an address

You can add a postal address and other contact details manually.

1 Click the ⋮ icon at the top right of Chrome and select the **Settings** option.

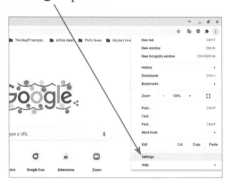

2 On the Settings page, select **Autofill** in the left-hand panel. Then, select **Addresses and more** from the section options.

Hot tip

The Autofill feature is turned **On** by default, but you can alter its settings to stop Chrome saving and filling address, passwords, and/or payment methods.

3 Under **Addresses**, you will see any addresses you have already added. To add a new one, click the **Add** button.

4 In the **Add address** dialog box, choose your country/region and then fill in the details for Name; Organization (if any); Street address; Town/City, State, ZIP code (or Postal town and Postcode); Phone number; and Email address. Then, click on **Save**.

Now, whenever you need to fill in a web form, Google will offer the option to fill in the saved address/contact details when you click in a field. Select the address to autofill the details.

Hot tip

Forgotten a password? If it's saved in Chrome, you can view it in **Settings** > **Autofill** > **Passwords**, by clicking the eye icon – you'll be asked to enter your Google account password first.

Beware

Before saving passwords and payment methods in Chrome, make sure you have a secure, unguessable password for your Google account. For added security, **2-Step Verification** is now turned **On** by default for Google accounts.

...cont'd

Saving passwords

Another very useful Chrome Autofill feature is the ability to save and fill in passwords – and usernames – for different websites (who on earth can remember them all?).

When you first enter your login details for a site, Google will ask if you want to save the password for it. If so, hit the **Save** button. The next time you log in to that site, Google will then autofill your login details, including the password.

Chrome may also suggest a strong password (made up of random letters, digits, and symbols for extra security) when you create a new account on a website. This is a good idea – with Autofill, you don't need to remember it!

You can manage your password list and settings in **Settings** > **Autofill** > **Passwords**.

Saving payment details

Autofill also enables you to save payment details, such as a credit card number and expiry date, so that you don't need to fill them in every time you buy something online – nor do you need to save them to a third-party website that may or not be secure.

When you first enter payment details on a site, Chrome will ask if you want to save them. If so, click **Save**. The next time you go to fill in

payment details online, Chrome will offer to autofill your card details. For security reasons, it will then prompt you for the CVC code for your card, which can usually be found on the back of your card.

You can manage your payment method list and settings in **Settings** > **Autofill** > **Payment methods**.

Using multiple windows

While you can create multiple tabs for sites in Chrome and group them together to organize them and also save space in the tabs bar when groups are collapsed (as we demonstrated on page 52), sometimes it can help to open a new window. For instance, you may want to keep all your work-related tabs in one window, and home-related ones in another.

Opening a new window

To open a new window in Chrome, click the **⋮** icon and select **New Window**. Alternatively, use the **Ctrl + Shift + n**  keyboard shortcut. A new window will open with the **google.com** page.

Closing a window

To close the currently selected window, click the **X** 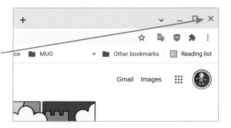 icon in the top-right corner (as with any other window in Chrome OS).

Switching windows

Press the ⊞ (**Show windows**) key and then select the desired Chrome window.

Alternatively, hold the **Alt** key and press **Tab** to switch between windows. Or, just click the Chrome icon on the Shelf and choose a window from the menu that appears.

Don't forget

You can also bring up **Overview** mode, showing all open windows and desks, by swiping up with three fingers on the touchpad.

Resizing windows

Resizing a window

To change the size of a Chrome window, simply hold and drag one of its edges or corners – just like any other window in Chrome OS.

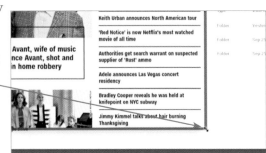

You will find the same window controls for every window in Chrome OS.

Window controls

To make the window full-screen, click the ☐ icon (**Maximize**) at the top right. To restore it to the previous size, click the ⧉ icon (**Restore**). To **Minimize** the window, click the — icon – to reopen it, click the Chrome icon on the Shelf and then select it from the menu that appears.

You can also zoom in and out of a web page using a spread/pinch gesture with your thumb and finger on the touchpad.

Zooming in and out

If the text on a web page is too small to read, or you want to get a closer look at an image, you can zoom in on the view by pressing **Ctrl** with the **+** key.

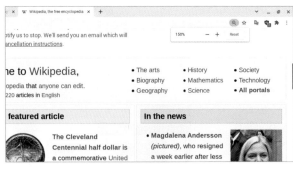

To zoom the page view out, press **Ctrl** with the **-** key.

To restore the page view to its standard 100% size, either press the **Reset** button in the zoom tool that appears under the Omnibox after pressing one of the zoom keyboard shortcuts or just press **Ctrl + 0**.

You can make everything on your screen bigger or smaller by pressing **Ctrl + Shift** and + or -. Reset the zoom level with **Ctrl + Shift + 0**.

Choosing a new theme

You can alter the look of the Chrome web browser by downloading and using ready-made themes or creating your own custom theme.

Using a ready-made theme

To use one of the many ready-made themes available, follow these steps:

1 Open the **Web Store** app from the Launcher to visit it in Chrome. Then, select the **Themes** section.

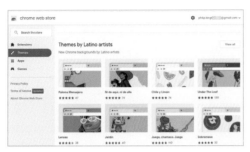

2 Scroll through the many themes and click on one you like. Click **Add to Chrome**.

3 Within seconds, the theme will be applied to Chrome. To view the theme background, open a new tab.

The installed theme may also be applied to Chrome on other computers on which you are signed in to your Google account. So, make sure you like it.

...cont'd

Reverting to the default theme

To remove a theme and return to the standard Chrome look, click **Undo** in the bar that appears just after installing it.

If the bar is not visible, go to **Settings** > **Appearance** and click the **Reset to default** button next to the **Browser themes** option.

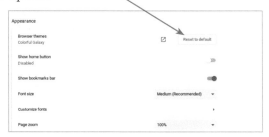

Creating a custom theme

You can also customize Chrome's appearance manually.

1 Open a new tab and click the pencil icon (**Customize Chrome**) at the bottom right.

2 In the dialog box that appears, click the **Color and theme** option on the left.

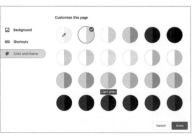

Hot tip

Once you have created a custom theme, only the pencil icon will be shown at the bottom right of a new tab.

3 If you want to use one of the color schemes shown in the circles, click on it.

Or, click the eye-dropper icon at the top left and choose your own base color: select a shade on the spectrum bar and then move the dot to adjust it. Then, click anywhere outside the box to apply the color.

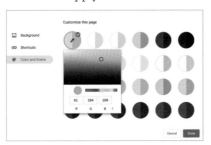

4 To add a custom background image, click the **Background** option on the left. Select an image from one of the collections or click **Upload from device** to use an image stored on the Chromebook.

The background will now be applied and your custom theme will be complete.

Changing the search engine

By default, the search engine in Chrome is Google. However, if you'd like to try a different one, it's very simple to switch. You will then use the chosen default search engine whenever you type a search term in the Omnibox or open a new tab.

Setting the search engine

To switch to a different search engine, follow these steps:

1 Click the ⋮ icon at the top right of Chrome and select the **Settings** option.

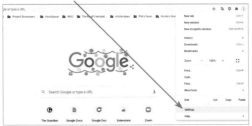

2 On the Settings page, click **Search engine** in the left-hand panel. You can select one of the options in the drop-down menu: Google, Bing, and Yahoo! by default.

3 Or, to add a different search engine, click **Manage search engines**. Under **Other search engines**, you'll see any other search sites you've used in Chrome; to use one, click ⋮ next to it, then **Make default**.

Hot tip

You can use an alternative search engine temporarily by typing its keyword (e.g. **bing.com**) followed by a space in the Omnibox. The keyword can be edited in the **Manage search engines** settings.

6 Communicating with Gmail

Email has been a useful and convenient communication tool for decades, and Gmail (formerly known as Google Mail) is the default email service for your Chromebook. In this chapter, we explore its many powerful features.

About Gmail

Gmail is the default email app on your Chromebook. Short for "electronic mail", email is a way of exchanging written messages – but, unlike an instant chat app, don't expect an immediate reply. The message you send will be stored in the recipient's mailbox and they may not read it straight away.

Gmail is a free "webmail" service from Google, available in numerous formats, so you may have used it before on another computer, tablet, or smartphone.

How is Gmail different?

If you've used other email applications such as Outlook or Mail on a Mac, you will find much of the core functionality of Gmail is quite similar. It does differ in a few ways, however, including:

- **Labels**. Most email applications use folders for you to organize your inbox. Gmail uses labels instead. The advantage is that you can assign more than 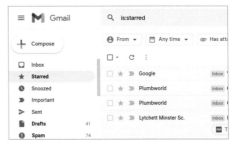 one label to an email message; it will then show up when any of those labels is selected in Gmail's left-hand panel. You can create your own custom labels, as we will explain later.

- **Stars**. You may be used to assigning color-coded flags (or categories) to mark messages in other email applications. Instead of flags, Gmail has a simpler system that allows you to "star" a message, which will then be assigned to the **Starred** label in the left-hand panel. If you really miss using multiple flags, you could use custom labels in place of them.

- **Importance markers**. Google automatically marks your email messages as important (or not) based on factors such as how often you email the sender, which messages you open and reply to, and keywords in emails that you usually read. You can adjust this manually by clicking on the $\sum$ important marker for a message or conversation, to mark it important or otherwise; this will help teach Google to mark new messages more accurately.

The user interface

Before we go into the details of Gmail's features and how to make the most of them, let's take a tour of its user interface:

Mailbox   Compose   Search bar   Status, Settings, apps

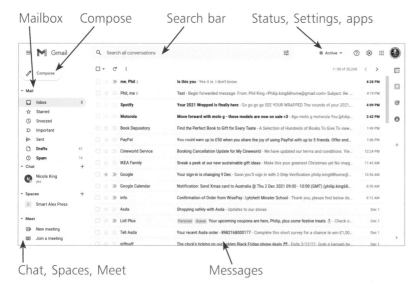

Chat, Spaces, Meet   Messages

- **Mailbox**. The left-hand panel shows all your Gmail system labels, categories, and user labels.
- **Messages**. The main panel shows all of your email messages for your inbox, or any other label or category selected in the left-hand panel. By default, Gmail groups messages and replies together in conversations.
- **Compose**. Click this button to start writing a brand new email message.
- **Search bar**. Type in a search term here to look for it in your messages. If you have a label selected in the left-hand panel, the search will be confined to it. The Settings icon on the right of the bar brings up an advanced search.
- **Status, Settings, apps**. Icons at the top include your status (e.g. Active) and Settings. Those at the side are for related apps such as Calendar, Keep, Tasks, and Contacts.
- **Chat, Spaces, Meet**. This area is reserved for Google Chat (for messaging), Spaces (for group chat), and Meet (for video chat).

Categories are built-in labels to filter certain types of messages: Social, Updates, Forums, and Promotions.

If you have chosen to hide some labels, you can still see them by scrolling down the list and clicking **More**.

Don't forget

Open the Gmail app from the Launcher, or visit **mail.google.com** in the Chrome browser.

Don't forget

For quick access, you can pin Gmail to the Shelf by right-clicking its icon in the Launcher and selecting **Pin to shelf**.

Hot tip

Icons at the top right enable you to print a message and open it in a new window. Under those are icons to star it and reply; click the ⋮ icon for additional options.

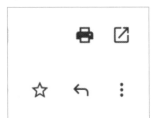

Viewing messages

The main panel of Gmail will show the messages you have received, filtered depending on which label you have selected in the left-hand panel. Preset system labels include:

- **Inbox**. Select this system label at the top of the left-hand panel to view all of your messages – except any that have been filtered as spam or by custom filters (see page 84).

- **Starred**. This label shows only messages that you have "starred" by clicking the star icon next to them.

- **Snoozed**. Messages that you have "snoozed" so that you won't see them in your inbox until later.

- **Important**. Messages that Google has marked as important, or you have marked manually – Google's AI learns from this.

- **Sent**. Messages you've sent to other people, including replies.

- **Drafts**. Messages you've started drafting, but haven't yet sent.

Reading an email

To read an email message, follow these steps:

1 Click on a message in the main panel. The view switches to show that message. Under the subject title, you'll see the sender's name and email address and to whom it was sent.

2 Scroll down to read the rest of the message. To close it, press the ← icon (top left) to go back to the inbox.

Writing and sending emails

Receiving emails is all well and good, but naturally you'll want to send them as well. You may want to compose a new email message to someone, reply to an email you have received, or forward it on to another person.

Composing a new email
To write a new email message, follow these steps:

1 Click on the **Compose** button (which also has a pencil icon) at the top of the left panel.

2 A new window will appear with **New Message** at the top. First, in the top field, marked **To**, enter the email address of who you want to send the message to. As you start typing, suggestions may appear from your Google Contacts list

(if you have any). Either select one of these or continue typing the desired email address.

3 In the **Subject** field, type a relevant subject (i.e. title) for the message. Then, write the message itself in the large field below. If you have the **Smart Compose** option turned **On**, you may see suggestions (akin to predictive

text) appearing as you type. To accept the suggestion, press the **Tab** key, or just carry on typing.

...cont'd

4 Finally, when you're happy with your message, click on the **Send** button to send it straight away to the recipient(s). Or, to send it at a later time, click the **Down** arrow on the button and select **Schedule send**.

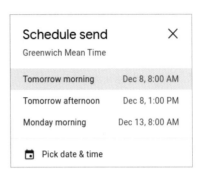

Extra options

Icons along the bottom of the window enable you to access several options for your email message, such as adding attachments and altering the text formatting:

- **Formatting options**. Clicking this option brings up a text-formatting toolbar at the bottom of the main message field. Clicking on an arrow icon will undo/redo the last change made. You can also choose a font and

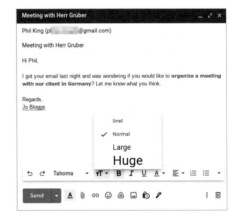

size; make text bold, italic, and/or underlined; choose a color for the text and background; align text to the left, center, or right; and add a numbered or bulleted list. Clicking the **Down** arrow on the right brings up more text-formatting options. To close the toolbar, click on the **Formatting options** icon again.

- **Attach files**. This option enables you to attach one or more locally stored (on the computer) files. Clicking it brings up a **File Manager** window; click on a file, hold **Shift** to select a range of files, or hold **Ctrl** to click and select multiple files manually. Click **Open** to add them to your message.

74

- **Insert link**. With some text selected in the message, click this icon to add a web link or email address to it.

- **Insert emoji**. Select from a range of emojis sorted into categories: face, object, nature, transportation, and symbol. Or, click the magnifying glass icon to search for one.

- **Insert files using Drive**. Select one or more files in your Google Drive, or any files or folders that have been shared with you by others. Use the search

field to help you find them. Click **Insert** to add them to the message.

Rather than adding the files to your message, the **Insert files using Drive** option adds links to them that the recipient can click on.

- **Insert a photo**. Add a photo from your account in Google Photos. The images shown in the selector window may have been taken on another device, such as a phone, signed in to the same account. You can also upload photos from your Chromebook or select a web address for an image online. You may insert images inline (embedded into the message) or as an attachment.

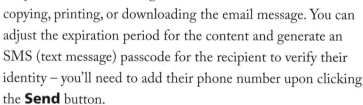

- **Toggle Confidential mode**. This option enables you to prevent recipients from forwarding, copying, printing, or downloading the email message. You can adjust the expiration period for the content and generate an SMS (text message) passcode for the recipient to verify their identity – you'll need to add their phone number upon clicking the **Send** button.

- **Insert signature**. Add a signature (with your job title, contact details, etc.) to the bottom of the email. For more details on how to create signatures, see pages 78-79.

Click the ⋮ icon to bring up additional options, including printing the message and spell-checking it.

Replying to or forwarding an email

You now know how to compose a brand new email message, but how about replying to one that you have received? Or, perhaps you want to forward it to a different recipient?

Replying to an email
Follow these steps to reply to an email you have received:

1 Click on the received email in the list in the main panel to open it. At the bottom, you'll see two buttons called **Reply** and **Forward**.

2 Click on the **Reply** button. A new panel will open up below the original message. The sender's name and email address will already be filled in, but you can add extra recipients by clicking in that field (which also brings up **Cc** and **Bcc** options).

3 Proceed to write your reply message in the main field. All the standard text-formatting options are available in a toolbar, including font, size, color, and alignment. You'll also find the usual icons underneath for various options (see pages 74-75 for details).

4 If you want
to pop the
panel out
into a new
window
to work
on your
message,

click the icon in the top-right corner of the reply panel.

If you close the message
window, the message
will be saved under the
Drafts label so that you
can work on it later.

5 You can press the ••• icon to see the original message
below the reply area.

Forwarding an email
To forward a message to someone else, follow these steps:

1 Click on a message in the list to open it. Click on
the **Forward** button at the bottom.

2 As with
a reply, a
new panel
will appear,
but this
time the
recipient
box will be empty. Enter the email address of the person
you want to forward the message to.

3 Again, you
have access
to all
the usual
formatting
tools and
other email
options. You
can also pop
out the message into a new window if you prefer.

You can forward a
message to multiple
recipients by adding
more addresses in the **To**
field (or **Cc** or **Bcc**).

Creating signatures

When you send email messages to people, particularly if they are work-related, you will probably want to put your details and contact information at the bottom.

Having to type all of this out manually every time you send a message would be laborious. Fortunately, Gmail enables you to store the information in a signature. You can create more than one signature for different purposes.

Creating a new signature

Just follow these steps to create a signature:

1 At the top right of the Gmail window, click the ⚙ **Settings** icon to open the **Quick settings** panel. Click on the **See all settings** button.

2 In the **General** tab of **Settings**, scroll down to find the **Signature** section and click on the **+ Create new** button.

3 Enter a name for the signature (e.g. "Work") and click the **Create** button.

4 Now, type your signature details into the text box. A toolbar below it gives access to all the usual text-formatting options. You can also add images and links if you want.

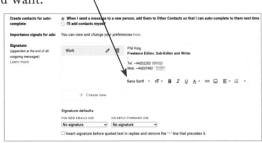

Hot tip

You can use the **Signature defaults** settings to determine the signature to use by default for new messages and replies/forwards.

Hot tip

There's also an option to insert the signature before quoted text and remove the "—" line that precedes it.

5 If you want to create another signature, click on the **+ Create new** button again.

6 When you're happy with the signature(s), scroll down to the bottom and click **Save Changes**.

Using a signature

When composing a new message or replying to one, click the **Insert signature** icon in the toolbar at the bottom, then choose a signature to add.

Editing a signature

If you want to edit an existing signature, follow these steps:

1 At the top right of the Gmail window, click the ⚙ **Settings** icon to open the **Quick settings** panel. Click on the **See all settings** button.

2 In the **General** tab of **Settings**, scroll down to find the **Signature** section, select the signature you want to alter, and edit the text box for it.

3 When you have finished editing it, scroll down to the bottom of the page and click **Save Changes**.

Deleting a signature

To delete a signature that you no longer need, select it in the **Signature** section of the **Settings** page. Click the trash can icon and then click **Delete** in the dialog box to confirm.

Adding and editing contacts

By default, any contact to whom you send a message will automatically be added to your Google Contacts (in the **Other contacts** folder) and be used for autocomplete suggestions for recipients. You can turn this option **Off** in the settings, however. You can also add and remove contacts manually.

Creating contacts for autocomplete
To alter whether people are added automatically to contacts when you send a message, do the following:

1 At the top right of the Gmail window, click the ⚙ **Settings** icon to open the **Quick settings** panel. Click on the **See all settings** button.

2 In the **General** tab of **Settings**, scroll down to find the **Create contacts for auto-complete** option. Then, click on one of the two options to enable/disable it.

Adding, editing, and removing contacts manually
To manually add, edit, and remove contacts, follow these steps:

1 In the right-hand panel of the Gmail window, click the **Contacts** icon (a person). Select the middle icon, **Open in new tab**, at the top of the **Contacts** panel.

2 Click on the **Create contact** button to add a new contact. Then, fill in their details.

3 To edit a contact, search for them and click **Edit**. To remove them, click the ⋮ icon and select **Delete**.

Hot tip

To add a contact quickly from an email message, click on their address to bring up a dialog box. Then, click the **Add to contacts** icon at the top right.

Organizing your inbox with labels

As mentioned previously, Gmail uses labels rather than folders to help you organize your inbox – something we all need to do to avoid missing important emails.

The advantage of using labels is that you can assign more than one to an email message; it will then show up when any of those labels is selected in Gmail's left-hand panel. You can also create your own custom labels, and even labels nested within labels.

Labeling a message
To add a label to an existing message, do the following:

1 Find the message in your inbox and click the box to the left of it – you can check boxes for multiple emails. Then, click the **Labels** icon at the top.

2 Search for a label or scroll down the list. Check the box for one or more labels, then click **Apply**.

3 The message will now show the label in its subject field. It will also appear in the list when you select that label in the left panel.

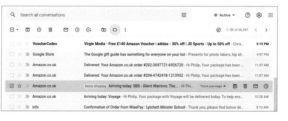

...cont'd

Creating a new label

You can also create your own custom labels. Follow these steps:

1 When adding a label to a message (see page 81), click on **Create new**.

2 A **New label** dialog box will appear. Type the name of your new label in the top field and click **Create**.

3 If you want to nest it under another existing label (akin to a folder within a folder), check the box and choose a label from the drop-down list.

Color-coding a label

You can add a color to a label to make it more visible.

1 Select the label in the left-hand panel and click the **⋮** icon, then **Label color**.

2 Choose a color from the grid or click **Add custom color** to create a new one.

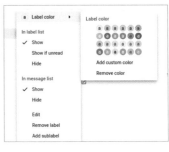

Hot tip

Alternatively, scroll to the bottom of the labels under **Mail** in the left panel and click **More**, then **Create new label** at the bottom.

Hot tip

You can choose to show or hide certain labels under **Mail** in the left panel. Go to **Settings** > **See all settings**, and select the **Labels** tab. Choose **Show**, **Hide**, or **Show if unread** for each label.

Searching for emails

Looking for that important email from your boss? Gmail's search function is your friend. You can search your entire inbox, within a particular label, or do an advanced search.

Basic search

With **Inbox** selected in the left panel, type a term into the Search box at the top to search all conversations for it. As you type,

suggestions will appear; choose one or press the **Enter** key to bring up all the results in a list.

Label search

To search for a message within a particular label, select the label in the left-hand panel. A condition – e.g. "label:notes" – will appear in the Search box. Type your search term in the box as usual.

Advanced search

To perform an advanced search, click the ☰ **Show search options** icon at the right of the Search box. You can then fill in a range of search options:

- **From**. The sender of the email.
- **To**. The recipient of the email.
- **Subject**. What's in the email's subject field.
- **Has the words**. Look for words in any part of the email.
- **Doesn't have**. Exclude emails with certain words.
- **Size**. The email size is greater or less than a certain number of MB (megabytes), KB (kilobytes), or bytes.
- **Date within**. Select a date from the calendar in the right-hand field, and the accuracy level in the left-hand field.
- **Search**. Choose **All Mail** or a particular label.

Check the box for **Has attachment** to only search for messages that have a file attached.

An advanced search can be used to create a filter. See page 84 for more details on filters.

Using filters

Filters are another useful tool to help you organize your emails. They can be set up to send certain emails to a label; or archive, delete, star them; or automatically forward mail.

Creating a filter
To create a new filter, follow these steps:

1 Click the ⯭ **Show search options** icon at the right of the Search box. You can then fill in a range of options, as covered on page 83. These are the rules used to choose emails to apply the filter to. When happy, click **Create filter**.

Hot tip

You can also create a filter based on an existing message. Check the box next to it in the list, then click the **⋮** icon and select **Filter messages like these**.

2 Now, you'll get to decide how to handle messages that match those criteria. Options include starring it, applying a label, forwarding it to a certain address, and marking it as important. You can also check the box at the bottom to apply it to any existing matching conversations.

Editing or deleting a filter
To see your filters, and choose to edit or remove them:

1 At the top right of the Gmail window, click the ⚙ **Settings** icon to open the **Quick settings** panel. Click on the **See all settings** button.

Hot tip

From the **Filters and Blocked Addresses** tab in **Settings**, you can check the box next to a filter and click **Export** to save it as an XML file. You can also import a filter from an XML file.

2 Select the **Filters and Blocked Addresses** tab. Find the filter you want to change and click **edit** or **delete**. If you choose **edit**, you'll be able to adjust the filter criteria and how matching emails are sorted.

84

Adding a task

Gmail is integrated with Google Tasks (selectable from the right-hand panel), which is a useful tool for creating to-do lists for all those things you need to do. Email messages in Gmail can be used to quickly and easily create new tasks.

Creating a task from an email

To add a new task to Google Tasks based on an email message, take the following steps:

1 Either check the box next to the message (or multiple messages) in the Gmail list or open the message. As when we were creating labels (on page 82), a row of icons appears along the top. Select the ✅ **Add to tasks** icon.

2 The right-hand panel will open and the task will be added to it. You can change the title if you want and add any extra details in the field below.

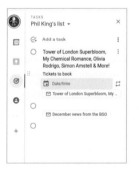

3 You can also set a date for the task. Click on **Date/Time** and then choose a date from the calendar, and click **Set time** to add a time for it if you want.

Hot tip

Setting a date/time will add the task to the Tasks calendar in your Google Calendar.

Archiving and muting messages

Want to tidy up your inbox, but don't want to delete messages? You can archive or mute them instead.

Archiving an email

Follow these steps to archive an email:

1 Either check the box next to the message (or multiple messages) in the Gmail list or open the message. A row of icons appears along the top. Select the ⬇ **Archive** icon.

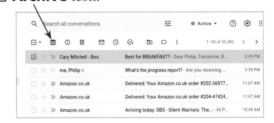

2 The message will be removed from the inbox and archived, but not deleted – you can still view it again later under the **All Mail** label or by searching. To unarchive it, select the message and then the **Move to inbox** icon.

Muting an email

Follow these steps to mute a group conversation so that any further replies from participants won't show up in your inbox:

1 Check the box next to the message in the Gmail list, or open the message. A row of icons appears along the top. Select the ⦂ icon and then **Mute**.

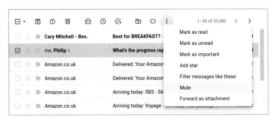

2 As with archiving, the message will be removed from the inbox, but not deleted – you can still view it again later under the **All Mail** label or by searching. To unmute it, click the ⦂ icon, then **Unmute**.

If you archive a conversation, any further replies will still appear in your inbox. If you don't want this, you will need to mute it.

Another option is to snooze an email conversation until a later time. See page 88 for more details.

Dealing with spam

One of the downsides of email is that you may be inundated with unwanted messages, known as "junk mail" or "spam". While Gmail is pretty good at filtering spam automatically, sometimes messages from valid senders may end up under the **Spam** label, so let's see how to correct that.

Showing spam label

While some email clients have a **Junk** folder, Gmail has the **Spam** label. This is hidden by default; to make it show up in the left panel, do the following:

1 At the top right of the Gmail window, click the ⚙ **Settings** icon to open the **Quick settings** panel. Click on the **See all settings** button.

2 Click on the **Labels** tab. Find **Spam** in the list and select the **show** option.

Retrieving an incorrectly labeled message

To move a message from the **Spam** label to the inbox:

1 Select the **Spam** label in the left panel, under **More**. If it's not there, follow the steps above.

2 Check the box for a message that you know isn't spam. Then, click the **Not Spam** option that appears. The message will be moved to the inbox and further emails from that sender should no longer be marked as spam.

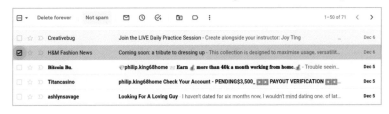

Beware

Note that some malicious spam emails may contain links to fake websites to "phish" for your login or payment details, so don't click on them! Attached files may also contain malware, so don't open them.

Snoozing an email

Sometimes you may not be able to deal with an email right away, but want to be reminded about it at a later time or date. This is where Gmail's snooze function really comes in handy.

Snoozing an email

Follow these steps to snooze an email or conversation:

You can also opt to mute or archive an email or conversation. For details, see page 86.

1 Either check the box next to a message (or multiple messages) in the Gmail list or open the message. As usual, a row of icons appears along the top. Select the **Snooze** icon (a clock face).

2 You will be presented with a list of times and dates to snooze until. You can select one of these or, to set your own custom one, click **Pick date & time**.

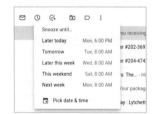

3 If you chose the latter option, you can then select the desired date and time from a dialog box with a calendar.

4 Either way, the snoozed message will be removed from your inbox temporarily and archived until the chosen date and time, when it will reappear in the inbox as if it had just been sent.

You can view snoozed messages under the **Snoozed** label. To unsnooze a message, select it, click the **Snooze** icon and then select **Unsnooze**.

Accessing Gmail offline

While you do require an internet connection to receive and send emails, you can still access your Gmail account when offline and also place messages in your outbox, which will be sent as soon as you're back online.

Enabling Gmail offline
To use Gmail offline, you'll need to enable the feature.

1 At the top right of the Gmail window, click the ⚙ **Settings** icon to open the **Quick settings** panel. Click on the **See all settings** button.

2 Select the **Offline** tab and check the box next to **Enable offline mail**.

3 Select how many previous days of emails you want to store for offline mode: **7**, **30**, or **90**.

4 Choose one of the security options; the first is recommended for smoother operation and less time resyncing afterward. Click on **Save Changes**.

Hot tip

When you go back online, Gmail will once again sync its mailbox with your Chromebook, observing any changes you have made while offline.

Accessing Gmail when offline
Once the offline functionality is enabled, as detailed above, you will be able to access your Gmail account when offline. Just open the Gmail app or visit **mail.google.com** in Chrome.

You can now access emails from the last however many days you set when enabling offline mode. You can also send a message, although it will be stored under the **Outbox** label and then sent as soon as you're online again.

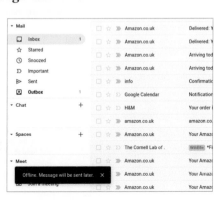

Instant chat

Sometimes, you may want to converse with someone without having to wait for email replies. For this purpose, you can use the Google Chat function to engage in instant messaging. It's integrated into Gmail and found in the left-hand panel.

Starting an instant chat

Follow these steps to use Google Chat for instant messaging:

1 In the left-hand panel of Gmail, under the **Mail** section, you will find **Chat**. Click the **+** button next to it to start a new chat.

2 Search for a person or select one from the **Frequent** list that may appear below.

3 Send them a message. Their status indicator will show whether they are active or away. You'll see their responses as soon as they're sent.

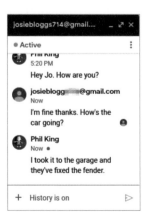

7 Google Drive

As a cloud storage service, Google Drive enables you to store your files online and share them easily with other people so that you can collaborate on documents. Find out how to make the most of Google Drive's features in this chapter.

What is Google Drive?

Google Drive is a cloud storage service – indeed, it's the most popular one in the world. Just like other similar services, such as Dropbox and OneDrive, it enables you to store your files remotely on a server elsewhere, "in the cloud".

This means that as long as you have internet access and are signed in to your Google account, you can access your files stored on Google Drive from any device, including a computer, tablet, smartphone, and, of course, your Chromebook.

Accessing Drive on your Chromebook

The easiest way to access Google Drive on your Chromebook is to launch it like you would any other app or Chrome shortcut. You should be able to find its icon in the Chrome OS Launcher at the bottom of the desktop: use a two-finger swipe-up gesture to scroll the Launcher up further to see the first "page" of apps in a grid format. If you can't see the Google Drive icon, search for "Drive".

Click on the Google Drive web shortcut icon to launch it. By default, this will take you to **drive.google.com** in the Chrome browser – so, you could instead just enter that URL in Chrome's Omnibox rather than looking for the web shortcut icon in the Launcher, if you can't find it there.

Installing the app

Once the Google Drive site is loaded in Chrome, you also have the option of installing the dedicated Chrome OS web app for Drive if you prefer. Just click on the ⊡ **Install Google Drive** icon at

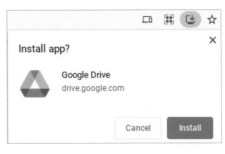

the right-hand end of the Omnibox. Once installed, clicking the app icon will launch it in its own dedicated Chrome OS window rather than Chrome, but the functionality is the same.

...cont'd

The user interface
Before we go into the details of Drive's features and how to make
the most of them, let's take a tour of its user interface:

New   Navigation sidebar   Ready for offline

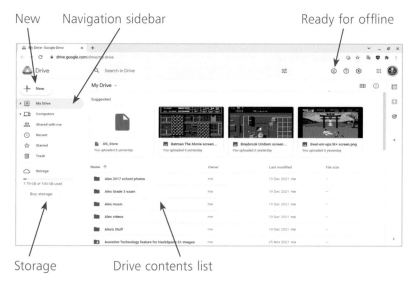

Storage   Drive contents list

- **Navigation sidebar**. This contains a range of categories to help you navigate Google Drive. **My Drive** is your home folder; **Computers** shows any other computers on which you have synced files to Drive; **Shared with me** contains files and folders others have shared with you; **Recent** shows newer files; **Starred** shows any you have starred; **Bin** contains unwanted files you've put there.
- **Drive contents list**. The main panel shows all the folders and files for the currently selected category in the sidebar. These can be ordered by **Name**, **Owner**, **Last modified**, or **File size**, by clicking the relevant heading.
- **New**. Click this button to upload a file or folder, or create a new document with one of the listed Google apps.
- **Ready for offline**. Click this icon to bring up the option for an **Offline preview**.
- **Storage**. This shows your remaining available Google storage. You can click **Buy storage** to upgrade your plan from the standard 15GB to 100GB or more.

Any documents you create in Google Docs, Sheets, Slides, etc. will be automatically stored in **My Drive**.

For more details on how to use Google Drive when offline, see pages 110-111.

93

Navigating files on Drive

Just like on a standard computer storage drive, your Google Drive files can be put into folders to help you stay organized. You can nest folders within other folders and even color-code them. You can also share your folders and files with other people who use Google Drive, and access those they have shared with you.

To color-code a folder, right-click it and then select **Choose color**.

Changing the view

By default, the contents of your Google Drive appear in the main panel in a list – with folders appearing first, followed by individual files. To switch to Grid view, click the ⊞ icon to the right of the bar below the Search field; files will then be shown in the main panel with a preview image.

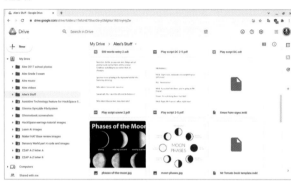

To switch back to List view, click the ☰ icon.

Searching for a file or folder

To find a file or folder anywhere in your Google Drive, simply enter a search term in the **Search in Drive** field at the top of the Google Drive interface. As you type, suggestions will appear below the Search field; click on one to go straight to it (such as opening a document), or continue typing your term and press **Enter** to bring up full search results.

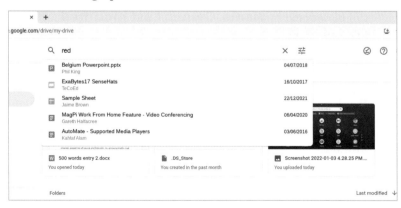

Advanced search

By default, the Search option looks for the term anywhere in files – so, for instance, it could be within the text of a document.

To help you narrow your search, you can use the Advanced search settings. Click on the ≆ icon at the right-hand end of the Search field to bring up a dialog panel.

Here, you can select various options to apply one or more filters to the search results, such as:

- **Type**. The type of file (or folder), such as a document, spreadsheet, presentation, photo, video, or PDF.
- **Owner**. The person the file belongs to; e.g. you, someone else, or a specific person.
- **Location**. Whether the file is in a specific folder, the Bin, or starred. You can also search for files available to people in your organization, if you are part of one.
- **Item name**. Enter a term that matches, at least partially, the file name.
- **Includes the words**. Search within documents for the specified word or phrase.
- **Shared to**. Enter a name or email address to match the person(s) with whom you have shared the file.

Once you are happy with the advanced Search options, click on the **Search** button at the bottom right of the dialog panel to view the results.

Creating and managing folders

As in any file system, folders are the key to keeping your files organized in a logical manner. Here, we'll show you how to create folders, as well as how to move files and folders around.

Creating a folder
To create a brand new folder in Google Drive:

1 Either select **My Drive** in the left-hand panel or open an existing folder if you want to store the new folder you will be creating within it.

2 Click on the **+ New** button at the top left of the Google Drive interface. Then, select the **Folder** option at the top of the list.

3 Enter a name for the folder and then click on **Create**.

You can share a folder, and all of the files within it, with other users. See pages 99-101 for details.

Hot tip

4 The new folder will appear in the list of contents in the main panel. If you had a specific folder selected before Step 2, the new folder will be a sub-folder within it.

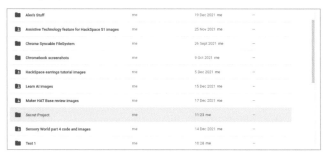

Moving a file or folder

There will be times when you want to move a file or folder to another place in the file system. There are two main ways of doing this. As on a standard computer file system, you can drag and drop the file or folder into its new location. If you want to move a file from one folder to another, however, it's easier to use the second method.

1 Right-click on the file or folder you wish to move. From the menu that appears, select **Move to**.

2 A menu will appear below the item. To select a folder outside of the current one, press the ← button at the top left to return to **My Drive** (or the enclosing folder if you are currently in a sub-folder).

3 At this point, you can select an existing folder from the list, or click the **New Folder** icon at the bottom left.

4 When you're happy with the location, click the blue **Move** (or **Move Here**) button at the bottom right of the menu. If you've made a mistake, just click on **Undo**.

Hot tip

Rather than moving an item, consider creating a shortcut to it that can be stored in **My Drive** or another folder. See page 98 for details.

Using shortcuts

Rather than moving a file or folder – or making a copy of it – you can create a shortcut link to it. This enables an item to appear in more than one location for easier access.

Creating a shortcut

To create a shortcut to a file or folder:

1 Right-click on a file or folder. From the menu that appears, select **Add a shortcut to Drive**.

Hot tip

If you want, you can create multiple shortcuts, in different locations, to the same item.

98

2 A menu will appear below the item. By default, **My Drive** will be selected, as this is where you will often want to place shortcuts for easy access. If not, press the **>** arrow next to it and navigate to the desired folder.

3 Now, click the **Add Shortcut** button at the bottom of the menu. The shortcut will be added – you can click **Undo** if you've made a mistake.

Using a shortcut

Shortcuts will appear in the Drive file system like a normal file or folder, but with a small arrow on their icons. Just double-click on a shortcut to open the linked file or folder.

Don't forget

Even if you delete a shortcut, the original file or folder will still be there.

If you want to find the original file or folder, right-click on the shortcut and select **Show file location**. You will then be taken straight to the actual item in the Drive file system.

Sharing folders and files

One of the key advantages of using a cloud storage service such as Google Drive is that it makes it easy to share your files and folders with other people so that they can view them, add comments, and suggest or make edits. This is very useful when collaborating on a document or project.

There are two main ways of sharing an item. You can either share it with selected people or get a link for it that you can share with others via an email message or other means. The latter can be more useful if you want to share something with a wider group of people and enable them to forward it to others.

Sharing a file or folder
To share a file or folder with selected people or groups:

1 Right-click on a file or folder. From the menu that appears, select **Share**.

To right-click on an item, you need to do a two-finger click of the touchpad.

2 A dialog box will appear with the option to share with people or groups, along with another to get a link for the item.

3 In the **Add people and groups** field, start typing the name of a person (or Google Contacts group/label) you want to share it with; suggestions from your contacts will appear, so select the relevant person.

4 You may add as many people as you like. They will appear at the top. By default, they will be permitted to edit the file or folder contents; to change this, click **Editor** and select **Viewer** or **Commenter** from the menu.

...cont'd

5 By default, the
Notify people
box will be checked,
which means they
will be notified of
the share via email.
You can also add an
optional message in
the field below.

6 Finally, click the **Send** button to share the item with
selected people. If one of the recipients has a non-Google
account, a warning box will appear – to send the share
invitation to them, click **Share anyway**.

Getting a link

As mentioned previously, another way to share an item with
others is to get a link for it that you can then email or send via
another communication method.

1 Right-click on a file or folder. From the menu that
appears, select **Get link**.

2 A dialog panel will appear with the automatically
generated link address filled in. Just click **Copy link** to
copy it to the Clipboard. You will then be able to paste it
into an email or other message.

3 By default, only people added in **Share with people
and groups** can open the link. If you don't want this,
click **Anyone with the link**.

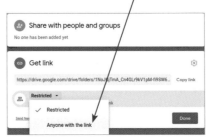

You can also bring up
the **Get link** panel by
selecting **Share** from
the right-click menu.

For an unrestricted link,
the default permission
level is **Viewer**, but
you can change this
by clicking the **Down**
arrow.

Stopping sharing

To stop sharing an item with someone:

1 Right-click on the file or folder. From the menu that appears, select **Share**.

2 Click on the **Down** arrow to the right of the person's permission level (e.g. **Editor**) and select **Remove**.

Shared folders in **My Drive** are indicated by a icon.

Changing the permission level

In the **Share** dialog, click on the **Down** arrow to the right of their permission level (e.g. **Editor**) and select a new one.

If you or your organization have a Google Workspace account, you'll find an extra permissions option to **Give temporary access** to an item.

Limiting how files are shared

You can prevent invitees from altering permissions and re-sharing. In the **Share** dialog, click the ⚙ icon, then uncheck the box for **Editors can change permissions and share**.

For a file, you'll also see a setting for **Viewers and commenters can see the option to download, print, and copy**.

Transferring file ownership

By default, the files and folders you create in Google Drive are owned by you, but it is possible to transfer ownership to someone else. This may be because you want to shift responsibility for a project to someone else.

Before you go ahead with transferring ownership, however, it's worth considering whether it might be better to simply share a folder with the person instead – with the default **Editor** option, they will still be able to share it with others and change permissions.

Transferring ownership
If you want to transfer ownership of an item:

Beware

You can't transfer ownership to a person with a non-Google account.

1 If you haven't yet shared the file or folder with the intended new owner, do so.

2 In the **Share** dialog panel for the item, click the arrow next to the person's permission level (e.g. **Editor**) and select **Transfer ownership**.

3 Another dialog will appear asking you to confirm. If so, click on the **Send Invitation** button.

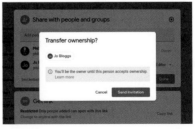

Hot tip

To cancel an invitation, click on the person's share permission again and select **Cancel ownership transfer**.

4 An email will be automatically sent to the person, inviting them to become the new owner of the file or folder. They can opt to accept or decline. Until they accept ownership, the item will still belong to you.

Seeing files shared with you

As well as the files and folders you have created yourself, Google Drive gives you access to any items that have been shared with you by other people.

These can easily be found in one place, or you can create shortcuts in **My Drive** for shared items. You can also opt to receive notifications in Drive whenever new items are shared with you.

Seeing shared items
To see all files and folders shared with you, simply click on **Shared with me** in the left-hand panel of Google Drive.

Creating a shortcut
You may want to add a shortcut in **My Drive** to a shared item. It's just like creating a shortcut for a standard file or folder.

1 Right-click on a file or folder, then select **Add a shortcut to Drive**.

2 A menu will appear below the item. By default, **My Drive** will be selected, but you can select another folder. Click the **Add Shortcut** button to confirm.

...cont'd

Getting sharing notifications

To be notified whenever an item is shared with you:

1 In Google Drive, click the ⚙ icon, then select **Settings**.

2 By default, the **Email address** option will be checked. To also get notifications in the browser, check the box for **Browser**, then **Allow** to confirm. You can check or uncheck boxes to choose exactly what you want to be notified about:

● **Newly shared items**. Be notified whenever new files or folders are shared with you.

● **Request for access**. Another user with a restricted link may send you a message requesting access to an item.

● **Comments, suggestions and action items**. Other users may add these to shared documents.

● **Approvals**. If you have requested approval of a document, it will show up here.

Removing a shared item

While shared items don't use up your Google storage allowance (see page 107), you may still want to remove certain ones. To do so, right-click on the file or folder and then select **Remove**. You can click **Undo** if you've made a mistake.

Note that removed items may still show up in Drive searches. Also, if you open a removed file (by visiting its link), it will show up in **Shared with me** again.

Uploading files to Drive

Documents that you create using Google Docs, Sheets, Slides, Forms, Drawings, etc. will automatically be added to My Drive in Google Drive. However, you can also upload locally stored files and folders to Google Drive manually.

There are two main ways to upload a file or folder from your Chromebook's local storage to Google Drive.

Uploading a file or folder from Drive
To upload items from within Google Drive:

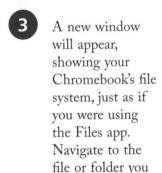

1 Click the **+ New** button at the top left of the Drive interface. Note: it doesn't matter which item you have selected in the left-hand panel, as uploaded items will automatically be added to My Drive.

2 Choose either **File upload** or **Folder upload**.

3 A new window will appear, showing your Chromebook's file system, just as if you were using the Files app. Navigate to the file or folder you

want and select it. You can select multiple files (or folders) by holding **Ctrl** or **Shift** as you click items.

4 Click on **Open** to confirm the upload. The window will close and a small box at the bottom right will show the items being uploaded – with a check mark symbol for each.

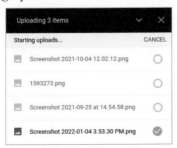

Hot tip

Uploading files to Drive is a good way to back them up. Alternatively, it can enable you to delete local files to free up storage on your Chromebook.

...cont'd

Uploading a file or folder from Files
The second uploading method is to use the Files app to copy locally stored items to Google Drive.

1 Open the **Files** app from the Launcher on the Chrome OS desktop.

2 Navigate to the file(s) or folder you want to upload to Google Drive. As before, you may select multiple files by holding **Ctrl** or **Shift** while clicking on them.

3 With the items selected, drag them over to **Google Drive** in the left panel.

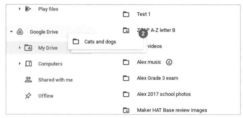

By default, items will be placed in **My Drive**. If you don't want this, click the arrow next to **My Drive** in the left panel, then the arrow next to that, and drag the items into the desired folder.

Dragging from Files to Drive
A variation on this method is to drag the files from the Files app into the Google Drive window. You can either drop them into a selected folder or above the Folders list to put them in **My Drive**.

Hot tip

Note that uploaded items will not be moved, but copied, so they will still be present in your Chromebook's local storage until you opt to delete them.

Hot tip

If you often upload files to the same Drive folder from the Files app, you may want to pin it to the top section of the left panel: right-click the folder and select **Pin folder**.

How Google storage works

With a standard Google account, you get 15GB of free storage. This may sound like quite a lot – and is more than you get with some other free cloud storage services. The downside is that this allowance isn't just allocated to Google Drive. Here's what counts toward it:

- Original-quality photos and videos backed up to Google Photos.
- High-quality/storage saver and express-quality photos and videos backed up to Google Photos after 1 June 2021.
- Gmail messages and attachments, which includes your Spam and Trash folders.
- Files in Google Drive, including PDFs, images, and videos.
- Files created or edited in collaborative content-creation apps like Google Docs, Sheets, Slides, Drawings, and Forms.

Note: Files uploaded or last edited before 1 June 2021 don't count toward your quota.

Checking and upgrading your storage

You can see your Google storage quota and the amount used at the bottom of the left-hand panel in Drive.

Underneath that is the option to **Buy storage**. Google One plans cost from $1.99/£1.59 per month.

If you have just bought a new Chromebook, you may be able to redeem an offer to get 100GB of storage free for 12 months – to check, open the **Explore** app and select **Perks** in the left-hand panel.

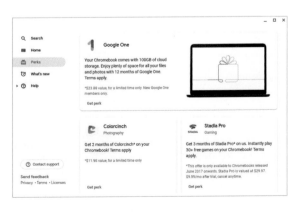

Freeing up space

As explained on page 107, you have limited free Google storage space. If you exceed the quota:

- You can't upload new files or images to Google Drive.
- You can't back up any photos and videos to Google Photos.
- Your ability to send and receive email in Gmail can be impacted.
- You can't create new files in collaborative content-creation apps like Google Docs, Sheets, Slides, Drawings, Forms, and Jamboard. Until you reduce your storage usage, nobody can edit or copy your affected files.
- You can't back up new Recorder files.

Freeing up storage space

To prevent this from happening, you can free up some Google storage space by removing inessential files from Drive.

1 In Google Drive, click on **Storage** in the left-hand panel.

2 A list will appear of files using Drive storage, arranged in order of size (largest to smallest, by default).

3 To remove a file from Drive, right-click on it and select **Remove**. It will first be moved to the Bin, but will still count toward your quota.

4 To remove it and free up the space, select **Bin** from the left-hand panel, then right-click the file and select **Delete forever.** Read the warning message and then click **Delete forever** to confirm.

Google storage space is in the cloud and is unrelated to the local storage capacity of your Chromebook.

Items shared with you don't count toward your Google storage quota.

Deleted files cannot be restored, so be careful! To be on the safe side, you could download the file to local storage first.

If you remain over the quota for two years, all of your content may be removed from Gmail, Google Photos, and Google Drive.

Using Microsoft Office files

If you have some Microsoft Office files, you may be wondering how to edit them on your Chromebook. It is possible to use the online Microsoft Office site, at **office.com**, if you have a Microsoft Online account. Alternatively, you can upload, share, and edit Office documents in Google Drive.

Uploading an Office document

You can upload Office documents just as you would any other files – see page 105 for details.

Editing an Office document

To open a Microsoft Office document in Google Drive:

1 Double-click on the file to open it in the equivalent Google app (e.g. Docs for a Word file). Or, right-click it and choose an app.

2 The file will retain its Office format; e.g. docx for Word, which is shown to the right of its name at the top.

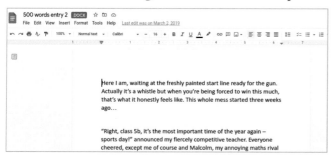

You can share an uploaded Office file like any other document in Google Drive – see page 99.

3 You can add comments on the side, which will appear in Office if you then download the file and open it there.

Converting a document to Google format

If you wish, you can convert an Office document to a Google one by saving it in the relevant format to Drive. For instance, for a currently open Word .docx file:

1 Click **File** > **Save as Google Docs**.

2 A copy of the file will be saved to Drive as a Google Docs document.

Accessing files offline

Since Google Drive is a cloud storage service that relies on an internet connection, you may be surprised that you can still access it when your Chromebook is offline.

It works by Google Drive automatically saving backups of recently opened and edited files to your Chromebook's local storage so that you can still access them when offline. There's also the option of making specific files available offline.

How to turn on offline access

To make Google Drive automatically back up recently used files to your Chromebook's local storage:

1 Before starting, make sure your Chromebook is currently connected to the internet. Check the Wi-Fi symbol at the bottom right of the desktop Shelf.

2 At the top right of the Google Drive interface, click the ⚙ icon and then select **Settings**.

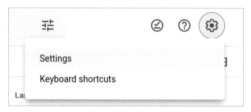

3 In the **General** section of the settings, scroll down to find the **Offline** option. Check the box for it to turn on offline access for recently used Google Docs, Sheets, Slides, and Drawings files. Then, click **Done**.

Only certain types of files may be accessed offline. You will also need adequate local storage.

Turning the **Offline** option **On** or **Off** will enable/disable offline access on all devices connected to Google Drive.

Making specific files available offline

You can also make a specific file available offline. This only works
for certain file types, including Google Docs, Sheets, Slides, and
Drawings, as well as Microsoft Office documents.

1 Before starting, make sure your Chromebook is currently
connected to the internet.

2 Right-click a suitable
file (see above)
and click on the
Available offline
option to make its
switch turn blue.

Enabling offline access
for specific files only
applies to them on the
current device.

3 A message in the bottom left of the interface will say
Making 1 file available offline (or a different
number if you have multiple files selected).

Making 1 file available offline ×

4 After a few seconds, a check mark symbol will appear to
the right of the file name in the Drive list to confirm it is
now available offline.

Offline preview

To quickly see which files are available offline, click the **Ready
for offline** icon at the top right of the interface. Any files that
won't be accessible offline will be grayed out.

Downloading files

Sometimes, you may want to download a file or folder from Google Drive to your Chromebook's local storage – so that, for instance, you can email it or back it up to an external USB storage device.

Note that downloaded Google Docs, Sheets, and Slides files will be converted to Microsoft Word, Excel, and PowerPoint files respectively.

Downloading a file
To download files from Google Drive to your Chromebook:

1 Select one or more files in the Google Drive interface – you can use the **Shift** or **Ctrl** key to select multiple files.

2 Right-click on the file to bring up the menu, then select the **Download** option.

3 You'll see a message in the bottom right saying that the file is being downloaded. In the case of multiple files, a zip file will be prepared.

4 Click on **Show In Folder** to see the file in your Downloads folder in the Files app.

5 In the case of multiple files, a zip file is downloaded. Double-click it to see its contents.

Only certain file types are downloadable, and they may be converted into a format that is readable on the Chromebook; e.g. to Word for a Docs file.

You can download a whole folder as a zip file, by right-clicking it and selecting **Download**.

8 Office and Productivity

A Chromebook can prove a cost-effective alternative to a Windows or Mac laptop for work. In this chapter, we explore how to use Google's suite of office apps, as well as how to organize your schedule and contacts.

Google Workspace apps

Formerly known as G Suite, Google's Workspace is an all-in-one office and productivity solution for individuals and organizations. Along with Gmail for email and Meet for video conferencing, it includes a range of office apps and productivity tools. While these are all free to use, Google offers a range of pricing plans for businesses to gain access to some extra services and features.

Before going into detail on how to get the most out of them, let's take a look at the main apps.

Office apps

Google Workspace features three main office apps that enable you to edit text documents, spreadsheets, and slide-based presentations. They can be opened from the Chrome OS desktop Launcher by visiting their URLs in the Chrome browser, or by opening or creating a new document from Google Drive.

The Workspace apps are all integrated with Google Drive. See Chapter 7 for more details on this cloud storage service.

Don't forget

114

Hot tip

Google Docs can also be used to open and edit files in other formats, such as Microsoft Word's .doc and .docx.

- **Docs**. Equivalent to Microsoft Word, this word processing application offers a similarly wide range of advanced formatting features. As with the other

office apps here, documents are stored in Google Drive – and, if the offline access mode is turned **On** (see page 110), copies of recently used documents are stored on the Chromebook so that you can continue working on them when offline.

- **Sheets**. Equivalent to Microsoft Excel, this is Google Workspace's application for working on spreadsheets. As such, it offers all

the advanced features with which you may be familiar, such as formulas, charts, pivot tables, and conditional formatting.

It can also be used to edit files in other formats, such as Microsoft Excel's .xlsx.

- **Slides**. Equivalent to PowerPoint, this is Google's application for producing slide-based presentations. As such, it offers a wide range of themes and fonts to choose from to fine-tune the look of your presentations. Advanced features enable you to embed videos and add animations.

Slides can also be used to edit files in other formats, such as Microsoft PowerPoint's .pptx.

Other apps and tools

Google Workspace also offers a range of productivity tools to help you stay organized and be creative:

- **Calendar**. Schedule meetings and events and get reminders about upcoming activities. It's also easy to share your schedule with other users and create multiple collaborative calendars.
- **Contacts**. This is where you can manage and organize all your contacts for use in other apps such as Gmail, Drive, and Meet. If you have an Android smartphone, they will also be synced there.
- **Keep**. This note-taking app offers a range of tools enabling you to quickly store text notes and lists, as well as images and audio. You can share them and sync them with other devices.
- **Forms**. Intended mainly for business use, this enables you to create custom forms for surveys and questionnaires.
- **Drawings**. Create charts and diagrams to add to your documents, presentations, and websites.
- **My Maps**. Create custom maps with the places that matter to you and share them with others.
- **Sites**. This tool enables you to create websites with no programming or design skills needed.
- **Jamboard**. An interactive whiteboard for jotting down your ideas, it can be used with others for a brainstorming session.

Third-party apps, Chrome extensions, and web services are also available, including **office.com** for editing Microsoft Office files.

Just like Google Drive documents, these websites can be shared publicly or with selected users.

Using Google Docs

The Google Workspace app you will probably be using the most, Google Docs is a word processing application for creating and editing text documents that – like those of other Workspace apps – are stored automatically in Google Drive. Let's take a tour of some of its most useful features.

Creating a document
To create a new document:

Don't forget

You can create a new blank document by entering **doc.new** in a Chrome browser tab.

1 Click on the  **Docs** app icon in the Chrome OS Launcher, or search for it.

2 Google Docs will open in a Chrome browser tab. In the **Start a new document section** at the top, either click on **Blank** or one of the templates available.

3 A new Docs document will be opened, ready for you to start typing. Any changes you make will be saved automatically in Google Drive.

4 To change the file's title, click on **Untitled document** at the top left and type a new name.

Text formatting

As with any word processing software, you can add formatting to your text. As well as adding bold and italics to words and phrases, you can use the formatting tools above the page to change the font, size, and alignment of the currently selected text, as well as a few other options.

To apply a paragraph style to create a title or heading:

1 With the desired text selected, click on the paragraph style box (which says **Normal text** by default) in the formatting toolbar.

2 Now, select an appropriate style, such as **Title** or one of the **Heading** options. The text will change to that style.

Hot tip

A host of different language letters, symbols, and arrows can be found by going to **Insert** > **Special characters**.

You can find extra styles by going to **Format** > **Paragraph Styles**. You can also alter the formatting for a style by first manually formatting some text and then selecting a style and the **Update to match** option.

If you click on **Show document outline** to the left of the page, the sidebar will show any headings you have applied; you can click on one there to jump to it in the document.

...cont'd

Adding an image

To add an image to your document:

1 Select a point in the document and click the ⊡ **Insert image** icon in the formatting bar, just to the left of the alignment options.

2 A menu appears with options for where to source the image. If you choose **Drive** or **Photos**, a preview of images will appear in a panel on the right. Select an image and then click **Insert**.

3 The image will be inserted into the document. You can resize it by dragging a corner or edge (although the latter will alter its proportions).

Collaborating on a document

One of the key advantages of working on documents based online, such as in Docs, is the ease with which you can collaborate with other users on them. First, you will need to share the document with the desired users, or share a link to it (see pages 99-100). Depending on their permissions level, users can then add comments, suggestions for edits, or make edits themselves.

Hot tip

To add a chart from a Sheets spreadsheet, simply copy it from there (**Ctrl + c**) and paste it into your Docs document (**Ctrl + v**).

Don't forget

Sheets is Google's spreadsheets app. To find out more about it, go to pages 120-123.

Adding comments or suggestions

To add comments or edit suggestions to a shared document:

1 Select some text in the document. Two icons will appear to the right: ⊞ **Add comment** and ◪ **Suggest edits**.

2 Choose ⊞ **Add comment** and then, in the box that appears, write a comment that other users of the document will be able to see and reply to.

3 Alternatively, choose ◪ **Suggest edits** and then make a suggested edit to the text. It's then up to the document owner to approve or reject the edit.

You can share any document in Drive with selected other users or publicly with a link.

Seeing version history

To view earlier versions of the current document, go to **File** > **Version History** > **See version history**, or use the **Ctrl** + **Alt** + **Shift** + **h** keyboard shortcut. You can then select a previous version and see the changes. If you want to restore the selected version, click the **Restore this version** button at the top.

Using spreadsheets in Sheets

Spreadsheets aren't just useful for doing your accounts: they offer a handy way of storing tables of related data in an organized fashion, as an alternative to a dedicated database, and can also be used to perform math calculations.

Google Sheets is a cloud-based spreadsheet application that makes it easy to share documents with other users.

Creating a document

To open a new spreadsheet document:

You can create a new blank document by entering **sheet.new** in a Chrome browser tab.

1 Click on the 🖽 **Sheets** app icon in the Chrome OS Launcher, or search for it.

2 Google Sheets will open in a Chrome browser tab. In the **Start a new spreadsheet section** at the top, either click on **Blank** or one of the templates available – you can click on **Template gallery** to see more options, which include a to-do list, budget, and calendar.

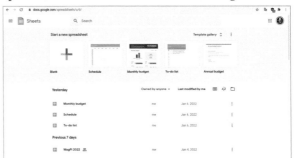

3 A new Sheets document will be opened, ready for you to start using. Any changes you make will be saved automatically in Google Drive. To give it a name, click on **Untitled spreadsheet** at the top left and type one.

…cont'd

Entering and editing data

If you are used to using Microsoft Excel or similar spreadsheet software, the way in which you enter and edit data in the cells is very similar.

1 Click in a cell of the spreadsheet and start typing text or numbers to enter it.

2 You can alter the cell's text or number formatting in the **Format** menu. For instance, to change a number to a currency, select **Format** > **Number** > **Currency**.

You can add various types of charts to sheets by going to **Insert** > **Chart** and selecting a data range and options.

Working with rows and columns

A spreadsheet is formed by numbered rows and lettered columns, so each cell has a location reference – for instance, C9 is in column C and row 9. These cell references are used in things like formulas, which we'll explore later.

To insert a new row above, or a column to the left of a cell, right-click the cell and then select **Insert 1 row above** or **Insert 1 column left**.

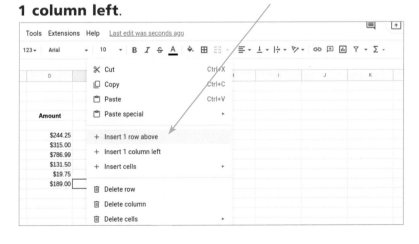

Alternatively, you can opt to **Insert cells** and shift the selected cell right or down.

...cont'd

Multiple sheets

A spreadsheet can contain multiple sheets, whose data may be inter-related using formulas. The names of the sheets are shown at the bottom; just click on one to switch to that sheet.

To add a new sheet, click on the **+** symbol at the bottom left. To rename it, click the **Down** arrow next to the sheet name and select **Rename**. You can also use this menu to **Duplicate** or **Delete** a sheet.

Using formulas

As well as entering data into your spreadsheet, you can use formulas to perform mathematical operations and other functions.

To enter a simple formula to add a column of numbers:

1 Click on the cell where you want the result of the formula to appear, then type **=**.

2 As we're doing a simple addition, type **SUM** after the **=**.

3 We now need to set the cells whose values we want to add together. Type a **(**, then hold and drag over the cells to use. In our example, this was D6:D11. Finally, add a **)** to complete the formula.

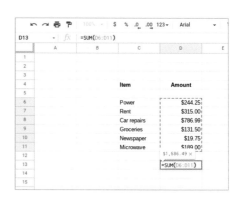

Hot tip

Upon typing **=**, you may be shown a suggestion for the formula, which you can accept by clicking on it.

4 Press **Enter** and the formula cell should now show the result of the addition. When the cell is selected, the formula will be shown in the formula bar above the sheet.

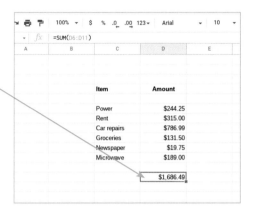

There's a huge array of other formula functions available, which you can explore by clicking the **Σ** icon in the toolbar above the sheet. They're sorted into categories such as Database, Engineering, Financial, and Statistical.

Conditional formatting

Another useful feature is the ability to apply special formatting to a cell that is conditional on the value within it – making it easier to see, for instance, whether a figure is over budget or not.

With a cell selected, go to **Format > Conditional formatting**. You can then select a rule from the **Format rules** drop-down list – for instance,

as **Less than**, with a value underneath. Only if the cell value meets this criterion will the formatting be applied.

You can switch from **Single color** formatting to **Color scale**, which will apply a different shade at different points of a value range. You can also create multiple rules for a cell.

Don't forget

You can share Sheets documents with other users by clicking **Share**.

Creating Slides presentations

Visual presentations comprising a series of slides have long been a favored way of showing a project to colleagues, promoting a product or service, or explaining how something works in a tutorial. There are many other use cases.

As a cloud-based app, Google Slides makes it easy to share presentations with colleagues and others.

Creating a presentation
To open a new presentation document:

Don't forget

You can create a new blank document by entering **slides.new** into a Chrome browser tab.

1 Click on the 📄 **Slides** app icon in the Chrome OS Launcher, or search for it.

2 Google Slides will open in a Chrome browser tab. In the **Start a new presentation section** at the top, either click on **Blank** or one of the templates available – you can click on **Template Gallery** to see more options. You can also change the theme later, in the document.

3 A new Slides presentation will be opened, ready for you to start using it. Any changes you make will be saved automatically in Google Drive. To give it a name, click on **Untitled presentation** at the top left and type one.

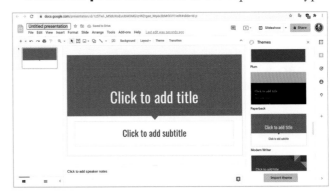

Adding text to your presentation

To add text to the current slide:

1 Click on the title, subtitle, or other text in the slide to change it. Type in whatever you like.

2 Clicking the icon to the left of a text box enables you to switch between autofit options. **Shrink text on overflow** will automatically adjust the font size to fit the text into the box if it's too long.

3 To add a new text box, go to **Insert** > **Text box**, then drag the cursor across the screen to draw the box.

Adding a new slide

A single slide doesn't make a presentation. To add another:

1 Click on the **Down** arrow next to the **+** button at the top left. A range of slide layout options from the current theme will be shown.

2 Click on one of the slide layout options to add it to your presentation. A thumbnail for it will also appear in the left-hand panel.

The text size and font can be altered manually by selecting the text and then using the options in the formatting bar.

You can resize existing text boxes in the usual way, by dragging an edge or corner.

...cont'd

Adding an image

To add an image to your presentation:

Don't forget

If you use an Android smartphone, any photos you take with its camera are uploaded to Google Photos by default.

1. Go to **Insert** > **Image**. A menu appears with options for where to source the image. If you choose **Drive** or **Photos**, a preview of images will appear in a panel on the right. Select an image and then click **Insert**.

2. The image will be placed in the slide. You can drag it from its middle to reposition it, and drag a corner to resize it while maintaining its proportions (dragging an edge will change them).

3. You can also crop a selected image by clicking the ⊡ icon in the formatting bar. Or, change the image to another by clicking **Replace image**.

Adding a chart

To add a chart to your presentation:

1 Go to **Insert** > **Chart**. Choose from **Bar**, **Column**, **Line** or **Pie**, or import a chart from one of your Sheets spreadsheets by selecting **From Sheets**.

2 If you chose one of the four preset options, click on the chart's top-right **Down** arrow and select **Open source**. You'll then be taken to a linked spreadsheet for the chart, where you can edit it and its data.

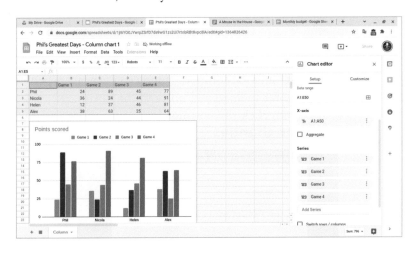

You can share Slides presentations with other users by clicking **Share**.

127

3 When you have finished editing, return to Slides and click on the chart's **Update** button.

Adding audio and video

You can add audio (from Drive) and embed video (from Drive, YouTube, or a URL) to your presentations via the **Insert** menu. For videos, you can choose a start and end time for playback.

To insert a diagram, go to **Insert** > **Diagram** and a panel will appear on the right with a variety of diagram categories; select one to see more styles. You can alter the number of levels and the color. On the inserted diagram, replace the dummy text with your own.

Viewing PDFs

PDF (Portable Document Format) files have long been a popular way of sharing documents that anyone can view, no matter which software was used to create them.

On your Chromebook, you can easily view PDFs, although the other options available are slightly different depending on whether they are stored locally or on Google Drive.

Viewing a PDF stored locally

To view a PDF stored in your Chromebook's local storage:

1 Open the **Files** app and navigate to the desired PDF file. Double-click it to open it in a Chrome browser tab.

2 As well as various view options, you can click the pencil icon to enter annotation mode. Here, you can use a pen and highlighter tools to add notes to the document. To save them, click the download icon and select **With your changes**.

Viewing a PDF on Drive

To view a PDF stored on Google Drive:

1 Open Google Drive and navigate to the desired PDF file. Double-click on it to open it in the same Chrome tab.

2 Unlike with the locally stored PDF, there are no annotation options – instead, you can add comments. Click the speech-bubble icon at the top right and then drag across the page to highlight an area and type your comment in the box that appears on the right.

When viewing a PDF stored in Google Drive, you can share it by clicking the **⋮** icon, then **Share**.

3 At the top, you'll also see an **Open with Google Docs** option. If you click this, it will open a new tab with the PDF converted to a Docs text document. Note that this may alter its appearance and layout.

Editing a PDF

While you could edit the PDF in Docs and then re-download it as a PDF file, it's also possible to edit it directly in a third-party app such as Lumin PDF or DocHub.

To do so, click the **Down** arrow next to **Open with Google Docs** to open an options menu and click on one of the suggested third-party apps.

You will be taken to the relevant app's site where you will need to grant it access to Google Drive to proceed. Some of the advanced features may require a paid subscription.

If the text is embedded as an image within the PDF, you won't be able to edit it.

Scheduling with Calendar

With the Google Calendar app, you can schedule meetings and events and get reminders about upcoming ones. Even better, you can share your schedule with other users and create multiple collaborative calendars.

To open Google Calendar, find it in the Launcher or open it from the right-hand sidebar in Gmail, Drive, or a Workspace app.

Day view calendar   Search contacts   Change to a different view

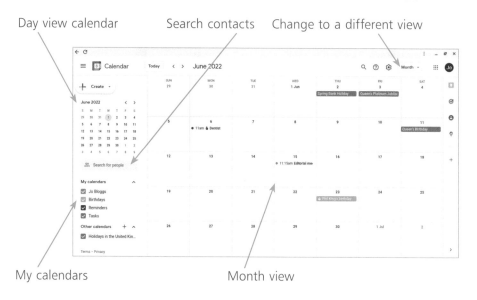

My calendars   Month view

The **Schedule** view shows a list of events from the currently selected calendars.

Check or uncheck the box next to each calendar in the list to show or hide it in the main panel.

- In the **Month** view, the main panel shows the days of the current month, and any events for them. Use the **<** and **>** arrow icons to move to the previous or next month.

- Click on this drop-down menu to switch to a different view, such as **Day**, **Week**, or **Year**.

- Clicking on a date here shows it in **Day** view in the main panel. Click on the date again to revert to the default view chosen in the top-right menu.

- Search for contacts to add to a new event or meeting.

- Your calendars are shown under **My calendars**. The top one will have your name and is your personal calendar. The **Birthdays** calendar shows any dates (such as birthdays) for people stored in your Google Contacts. The **Tasks** calendar shows any tasks created in Google Tasks. Any new calendars you create, or that are shared with you, are also shown in this list.

Creating an event

To add a new event or meeting to your calendar:

1 Click on the **+ Create** button at the top left, then select **Event**. A new window will appear for you to add details of the event.

2 Add a title at the top, then choose a date and time. You can also set a time zone if you are inviting international guests to a meeting.

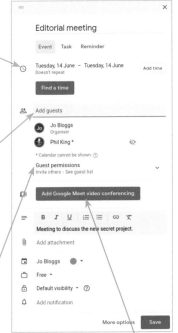

3 In the **Add guests** field, start typing the name or email address of a guest. If they are in your contacts, a suggestion will appear; click on it to add them. Alternatively, enter their full email address and press **Enter**. Under **Guest permissions**, you can alter whether they can modify the event, invite others, and see the guest list.

4 If you are scheduling a video meeting, click on the **Add Google Meet video conferencing** button. This will create a unique URL for the meeting, which will be shared with guests. If it's a real-life meeting, you can add the venue in the **Add location** field instead.

5 You can also add a description for the event and alter your own notification(s) for it – the default is 30 minutes before the event.

6 Click on **Save** and then **Send** to email an invitation to any attendees you have added.

The **Find a time** option enables you to check colleagues' calendars (if you have permission) to find out when they are all free for a meeting.

131

When guests receive an invitation, they are asked to confirm whether they can attend (**Yes**, **Maybe**, or **No**). When you view the event in your calendar, a check mark will be next to the names of persons answering **Yes**.

...cont'd

Creating a reminder

To add a personal reminder to the calendar:

1 Click the **+ Create** button and select **Event**, or click on a date in the main Calendar panel. A new event window will appear.

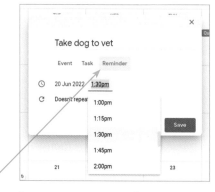

2 Add a title, then click on **Reminder** underneath it to change the event to a reminder.

3 If you need to add a time, uncheck **All day** and then click on the time to change it.

4 Click on the **Save** button to save the reminder. It will show up in the main panel – so long as the **Reminders** calendar is checked under **My calendars**.

Creating a task

Any tasks created in Google Tasks (accessible from Calendar's right-hand sidebar) will show up in the **Tasks** calendar when it is displayed by checking it under **My calendars**.

Alternatively, you can create one from Calendar:

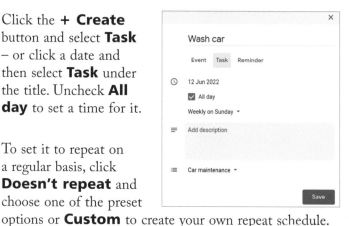

1 Click the **+ Create** button and select **Task** – or click a date and then select **Task** under the title. Uncheck **All day** to set a time for it.

2 To set it to repeat on a regular basis, click **Doesn't repeat** and choose one of the preset options or **Custom** to create your own repeat schedule.

Hot tip

To mark a reminder as done, click on it and then select **Mark as done**.

Hot tip

Tasks can contain subtasks, but you'll need to create these within Google Tasks.

3 Add an optional description and, if you have created any lists in Google Tasks, choose one from the bottom menu.

Sharing a calendar

One of the best things about Google Calendar is the ability to share calendars with colleagues, family, or friends for joint use.

To create a new calendar and share it:

1 Click the **+** button next to **Other calendars** at the bottom left and select **Create new calendar**.

2 In the **Settings** page that appears, give the calendar a name and optional description. Set the time zone and click **Create calendar**.

3 After a few seconds, it will be created and appear in the list on the left (still in **Settings**). Select it and scroll down to find the **Share with specific people** setting.

4 Click on **+ Add people** and add them by name (for contacts) or email address. If you want them to be able to modify and add events, click on the **Permission** box and set it to **Make changes to events**.

5 When you click **Send**, they will receive an email inviting them to add the shared calendar.

To mark a task as done, click on it and then select **Mark completed**.

To share an existing calendar, click the **⋮** icon next to it under **My calendars** and select **Settings and sharing**.

133

Managing contacts

Your contacts in Google Contacts are integrated into other Google Workspace apps, including Gmail, Drive, Calendar, and the office apps. This makes it easy to select them and share items.

Adding a contact

You can add a contact from Gmail, or within the Google Contacts app. To open the latter, search for it in the Launcher or visit **contacts.google.com** in Chrome. Click **+ Create contact** at the top left. Then, fill in their details and click **Save**.

Editing a contact

To edit an existing contact, use the Search facility at the top of Google Contacts or scroll through the list. Click on their name and then **Edit**. Alter their details and click **Save** (or the top-left **X** icon to discard changes).

Hot tip

To resolve duplicate contacts, click on **Merge and fix** in the left panel.

Organizing contacts with labels

To make it easier to view and organize contacts, you can assign them to labels. To create a new label, click on **+ Create label** in the left panel, then give it a name and click **Save**.

Hot tip

To customize the view of the Contacts list, click the ⋮ icon at the top right and select **Change column order**.

To add a contact to a label, drag their name from the list to the desired label in the left panel. Alternatively, view the person's profile, click the **Manage labels** icon under their name, check a label and click **Apply**.

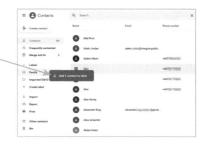

Note that, as with emails in Gmail, you can assign a contact to more than one label.

You can also star a contact to make them appear in the **Starred Contacts** section at the top of the list.

9

Media and Entertainment

All work and no play isn't good for you. Fortunately, your Chromebook can be used for a variety of leisure activities including watching movies and TV, listening to music, playing games, and reading books. Time to have some fun...

Uploading and organizing photos

You can double-click images stored locally on your Chromebook to view them in the Gallery app, which includes basic editing tools to crop, rotate, rescale, annotate and alter the lighting. Third-party apps such as Polarr offer more advanced editing options.

For organizing and backing up your photos, it's best to upload them to Google Photos. Also, if you have an Android smartphone, any photos taken with it will be synced automatically to Google Photos by default.

Uploading a photo or video
To upload an image from your Chromebook to Google Photos:

1 Click on the Google Photos app icon in the desktop Launcher, or search for it. A new Chrome tab will open at the address **photos.google.com**

The **Upload** menu also lets you add photos stored in Google Drive.

2 Any photos or videos already uploaded from any device will show in the main panel. At the top right, click the **Upload** button and select **Computer**.

You can select multiple files to upload by holding down the **Ctrl** or **Shift** key.

3 Navigate to the desired image file in your Chromebook file system, select it, and click **Open**. The photo will be uploaded to Google Photos, where a preview of it will appear at the bottom left – with options to add it to an album or a shared album.

Searching for a photo
Google Photos features a Search field at the top. Type a term here, such as a person, location, topic (e.g. Christmas), or even an item in the photo (e.g. ball), and press **Enter** to search for it.

Exploring options

Click on **Explore** in the left-hand panel to explore your photo library by **People**, **Places**, and **Things**. While locations may be added automatically when taking photos with a smartphone, Google Photos uses AI to identify people and objects. To add a name to an identified face so that you can search for them:

Beware

Uploading photos and videos to Google Photos counts toward your Google account storage quota – see page 107 for details.

1 On the **Explore** screen, click on one of the unnamed faces under **People** to see all photos with them in it. Click on **Add a name** at the top left, then type the person's name and click **Done**.

2 Click the ← arrow icon (or key) to return to the **Explore** screen, and their face will now have their name under it.

3 If Google has automatically created multiple sets of photos for the same person in **People**, click on one of the unnamed ones and enter their name; if it has been used for another set, you will be asked: "Are these the same face?" Click **Yes** to merge their photo sets into one.

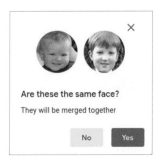

Correcting misidentification

Google's AI is pretty smart, but if it has misidentified something in a photo you can rectify this by doing the following:

1 After clicking on the person, place, or thing on the **Explore** screen, select one or more misidentified photos by clicking on their top-left check mark symbol.

...cont'd

2 Click the **⋮** icon in the top right and – for People and Things – select the **Remove results** option. You can give feedback and then **Submit** or just click **Skip**.

3 If correcting a wrong Place, however, from the **⋮** menu, select **Edit location** and enter the correct one.

Organizing photos with albums

Just like with traditional printed images, photos can be organized into albums to peruse. To create a new album:

1 Click on **Albums** in the left panel to see all your existing albums. To create a new one, click **Create album** and give it a name.

2 Click on **Add photos**, then select some by clicking their top-left check mark symbol and click **Done**.

Sharing and collaborating on albums

To share an album:

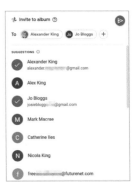

1 Select an album to view it. Click the **Share** icon at the top right and choose one or more contacts to invite. Then, click the **Send** icon at the top right.

2 The contact's photo/avatar will appear next to yours under the album title. They can now view, comment on photos, and – by default – add new photos to the shared album.

You can also share individual photos by selecting one or more photos and clicking the **Share** icon.

3 To prevent invitees from adding their own photos to the album, click the **⋮** icon, then **Options**, and turn off the **Collaborate** option.

Editing tools

When viewing a photo, click the **Edit** icon to apply filters, alter image settings, and crop and rotate. Then, click **Done**. You can revert it to the original by clicking **Undo Edits**.

You can see all shared albums and images by clicking on **Sharing** in the left-hand panel.

Utilities

Click on **Utilities** in the left panel to find the following options:

- **Create new Movie, Animation, or Collage** (automatically from selected photos) – This will prompt you to turn on the

  Creations setting. Once it has been created, which may take a while, the item will appear on the **Utilities** screen.
- **Move photos to archive** – This doesn't delete them, but means they aren't shown in the timeline on the standard **Photos** screen – they may still appear in albums and search results.
- **Assistant** – This panel may suggest rotating images that appear sideways. Click any wrongly auto-rotated image to correct its rotation, then select **Save All**.

After selecting one or more photos, click the **+** icon to add them to an album, shared album animation, collage, or movie.

Watching Google TV

The Google TV service enables you to watch movies and TV shows you have purchased or rented from its shop (or from the Play Store on an Android smartphone or tablet). Google TV also acts as a hub for other streaming services.

Launching Google TV
To start using Google TV:

1 Find the **Google TV** app in the Launcher or search for it there. If you have the Google Play Movies & TV app installed instead, launch that and you'll then be prompted to launch Google TV from it.

2 When the Google TV app launches, you may be prompted to add some of your streaming services to it – what

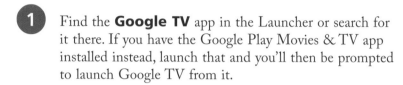

appears here will depend on your country of residence and any streaming services you have used in Chrome or on an Android device. Check the boxes to add them.

3 The Google TV interface will then appear, showing a range of movies and TV shows.

The Google TV interface

Don't forget

You can also watch streaming services from their websites or by using their Android app (if they have one) from the Play Store – see Chapter 10.

1 Scroll up and down (with two fingers) to see different categories. For each one, scroll left and right to view its "carousel" of movies and/or shows.

2 Click the ⚲ icon at the top left to enter a search term. It could be a movie/show title, actor's name, or topic (e.g. classic family movies). You can filter the search results by clicking the buttons that appear: **Movies** or **Shows**, **Free** or **Rent & buy**.

3 Switch between the three tabs at the top: **For you** suggests content you might like, based on your previous viewing history. The **Movies** and **Shows** tabs filter the content to that type of content.

4 Switch between the main **Home** screen, **Shop** (to buy content), **Library** (purchased content), and **Watchlist** (add to it by clicking an item's bookmark icon).

You'll need a payment method added to your Google account to be able to make purchases in Google TV.

141

Watching a movie or show
To start watching something:

1 Click on a movie or show in the interface to reveal details about it. Scroll down to see a white bar with the service name and **Buy/Rent** or **Watch now**.

The Big Leap

In Google TV and other video-streaming apps, click the ⌁ icon to start casting the video to another display.
For more details, see pages 172-173.

2 Clicking **Watch now** will prompt you to install the relevant streaming service app (if not already installed). You can then watch the movie/show in it. In future, some apps will launch automatically when you click on a movie/show; others require you to click on the white bar from the details screen.

Netflix streaming

Some streaming services are not yet available via the Google TV app, the most notable being Netflix.

For this, and most other services, you have the choice of watching via the Chrome web browser or the service's Android app (if it has one). We'll explore both options here for Netflix, but the process should be similar for most services.

Watching Netflix in Chrome

To watch using the Chrome web browser:

1 Open the **Chrome** app from the Launcher and enter "netflix.com" in the Omnibox at the top to go to the Netflix website.

2 If you haven't watched Netflix in a Chrome browser on any device previously and saved the password, you

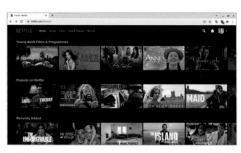

will be prompted to log in – or create a new account if you are not yet a subscriber.

Watching Netflix in the app

To watch using the Android app:

1 Open the **Netflix** app from the Launcher. If not yet installed, open the **Play Store** app and install it.

2 You will be prompted to log in to your Netflix account or create a new one if you're not yet a subscriber.

Hot tip

While both viewing methods offer a similar experience, the advantage of the app is that it allows you to download content to watch offline.

142

Viewing YouTube videos

YouTube can be viewed in two main ways: via Chrome or its progressive web app (PWA), or by using the Android app. The latter enables you to download certain videos for offline playback.

Watching YouTube in Chrome/PWA

To watch videos using the Chrome browser:

1 Search for YouTube in the Launcher, or open Chrome and visit **youtube.com**
If you've used YouTube before, you'll find suggested videos at the top. From the left-hand panel, you can view your channel **Subscriptions**. The **Your movies** option reveals any movies and shows you've purchased in Google TV or from the Play Store.

2 By clicking in the Omnibox, you'll also see an option to **Install YouTube**. If you do so, when you select **YouTube** from the Launcher  in future, it will launch the PWA instead of Chrome.

Watching YouTube in the Android app

To watch videos in the Android app:

1 Open the **Play Store** from the Launcher and install the YouTube app. Open it and you'll find that the interface is different from the website and PWA.

2 You can also download any content you've purchased from Google TV or the Play Store, in **Your movies and shows**, along with many other videos if you have a YouTube Premium subscription. Just click the **Download** button for a video; once downloaded, it will appear in the **Downloads** section in the **Library**.

Listening to music

Whatever type of music you enjoy, you can listen to it on your Chromebook. Locally stored music files such as MP3s can be played using the pre-installed Gallery app.

You can also listen to music on a streaming service such as with Google's YouTube Music app. Services such as Spotify, Amazon Music, Apple Music, and Deezer have their own Android apps.

If you don't want to listen using your Chromebook's speakers, you can plug in headphones, connect them (or a speaker) via Bluetooth, or cast the audio to a Google Nest smart speaker.

Listening to YouTube Music

To listen to tracks in YouTube Music:

1 Find the **YouTube Music** app icon (for the PWA version) in the Launcher and click on it to launch it.

2 If this is your first time in YouTube Music, you'll be asked to pick five artists you like (so that the app can make suitable listening recommendations). You can select more if you like, then click **Finished**.

3 The **Home** screen shows your favorite artists along the top. Click on one to see all their songs, albums, singles, and videos. Click on a song to play it, or an album to reveal its tracks.

Discovering new music

There are multiple ways to discover new songs and artists in YouTube Music:

Hot tip

To cast audio to a Google Nest smart speaker or compatible smart TV or device, click the ⛰ icon at the top right. For more details, see pages 172-173.

Hot tip

To use wireless headphones or speakers, see the guide to connecting Bluetooth devices on page 178.

Hot tip

If you don't have the YouTube Music app, go to **music.youtube.com** in Chrome, click in the Omnibox and then on the **Install app** icon.

- **Explore**. Click on this option at the top of the interface to find new releases that may be of interest to you, along with moods and genres, trending tracks, and new music videos.
- **Search**. Click the 🔍 icon at the top of the interface to search for a track or an artist.
- **Song radio**. The **Home** screen contains a **Quick picks** section to "start radio based on a song" from one of your favorite artists or associated ones. Clicking on one starts a playlist containing similar songs from various artists. You can also start song radio from any track: hover the pointer over it, click the ⋮ icon, and select **Start radio**.

Playlists and Library

As with other music-streaming services, you can create your own custom playlists (akin to mixtapes) of your favorite tracks or based on a theme. Click on the ⋮ icon for a song and select **Add to playlist**, then choose an existing one or **New Playlist**.

You can see all of your playlists on the **Library** screen, along with **Albums**, **Songs**, and **Artists** – the **Subscriptions** tab shows any artists to whom you have subscribed by pressing the **Subscribe** button on their artist page.

As with YouTube, you can also install the Android app for YouTube Music from the Play Store. For more details on installing apps, see Chapter 10.

Uploading your own tracks

You can upload songs from your personal music collection to YouTube Music. Click on your avatar at the top right, then select **Upload music**. Select one or more files from your Chromebook's file system and click **Open** to upload. Uploaded albums and songs can be found in the **Library**.

145

Playing games

It's possible to play a wide range of games on your Chromebook, in a variety of ways. In Chrome, you can play free web-based games by visiting online games websites such as **newgrounds.com** and **addictinggames.com**

Alternatively, you can use Google's Stadia app to play a wide range of games. You'll need an internet connection as it's cloud-based, with the games based on a remote server rather than on your Chromebook. While a Stadia (or PlayStation or Xbox) controller is advised, you can play many games with your touchpad and keyboard.

Last but not least, there's the option of installing Android games from the Play Store. While some must be purchased, others are free but may offer in-app purchases. With most Android games, you'll be able to continue playing when offline.

Playing games with Google Stadia
To start using Google Stadia:

1 Find the **Stadia** app in the Launcher, or search for it. Click on it to launch it.

2 Click the **Sign in** button to sign in with your Google account, then click **Confirm**.

3 Scroll down and accept the terms of service, then choose an avatar and Stadia username (not your own) – a number will be added to it to make it unique.

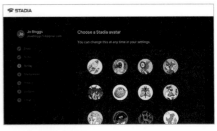

4 Select privacy and update options as you wish. You will then be offered a free trial for Stadia Pro – this subscription service allows you to play a much wider range of games without purchasing them. You will need to click **Start trial** and add a payment method to continue; you can cancel the subscription at any time.

Hot tip

To cancel your Stadia Pro subscription, click your avatar from the **Home** screen, select **Stadia settings**, then **Purchases & subscriptions**, and click **Unsubscribe**.

5 You will be invited to claim some free games as part of your Stadia Pro subscription, so click on the **Claim all**

option. Scroll down to **Your library** and click **See all** to see all of your games.

You can use your Stadia account on other devices, including other computers, smartphones, and Chromecast with Google TV.

6 Click on a game to see screenshots and/or a trailer video. Scroll down to view more details. Press the large glowing **Play** button to start playing the game.

To pause the current game, press the **Esc** key. To exit it, hold down **Esc** until a dialog appear, then select **Exit game**.

7 At any point, you can bring up a side menu by pressing **Shift** + **Tab**. In the **Friends** tab, you can find or invite friends to add to your friends list. In **Messages**, you can send messages to organize multiplayer game sessions. Click **Parties** to see available multiplayer games. Clicking on **Live stream** enables you to live-stream your gaming sessions to YouTube.

Playing Android games

You can play most Android smartphone games on your Chromebook, although a few may not be compatible or installable. Once installed via the Play Store app, they will appear in the Launcher grid menu. Click on one to play it. For more details on how to use Android games and apps, see Chapter 10.

E-books and audiobooks

There's nothing quite like settling down with a good book. You can read e-books on your Chromebook and also listen to audiobooks. The default app is Play Books, but you can also install Android apps such as Kindle for Amazon e-books, Libby and BorrowBox for libraries, and Audible for audiobooks.

Reading with Play Books

To start reading books with Play Books:

1 Find the **Play Books** app in the Launcher, or search for it there. Click on it to launch it.

2 The **Home** screen shows various categories of books available. Scroll down to see more; some may be based on your previous purchases. Click on **Ebooks** or **Audiobooks** to view each content type.

3 The **Shop** screen enables you to buy e-books and audiobooks. Click on one and you can get a **Free sample** or opt to **Buy** it for the price shown.

4 Your purchases are shown on the **Library** screen. They can be organized using **Shelves**. Click on a book to start reading it – it will download automatically.

5 Use two-fingered touchpad swipes right and left to turn the pages. Click in the middle to bring up an overview where

you can search the text and adjust display options (via the **Aa** icon) such as text size, viewing theme, and a **Night Light** that makes the screen easier on your eyes.

Hot tip

Clicking on a purchased audiobook brings up an audio player screen where you can skip forward and back and adjust the playback speed.

Hot tip

Click the ⋮ icon on the overview screen to find options such as adding a bookmark and reading a book aloud using synthesized speech.

10 Adding and Managing Apps

To make the most of your Chromebook, you will want to install additional apps. In this chapter, we explain how to do so from different sources, along with how to manage and update installed apps.

Progressive web apps

A progressive web app (PWA for short) is a relatively new type of app that is built from web technologies, so it can run on different computers and devices but behaves much like a native app. While a few PWAs may be found in the Play Store, such as Zoom for Chrome, most can be installed by visiting the relevant website.

Installing a PWA from a website
To install a PWA:

1 Open the **Chrome** app and visit a website that offers a PWA, such as **twitter.com**

2 Click in the Omnibox at the top and you should see a ⬇ icon on the right side of the box. Hovering the pointer over it will show a screen tip such as **Install Twitter**. Click on the icon to install the PWA for the site.

Hot tip

Other PWAs include SoundSlice, Pinterest, and SoundCloud. For a good list, visit **bit.ly/pwa-list**

3 In some cases, such as for Google sites, it will install straight away. For this one, it directs you to the app in the Play Store. Click on the **Install** button and it will install the PWA version since you are using a Chromebook.

Hot tip

If you subsequently visit the Twitter website, it will ask whether you want to open it with the app or in Chrome.

4 Once it has installed, the button will change to **Open**. Click on it to launch the app. It appears in its own window, just like a native Chrome OS or Android app. Its icon will also be added to the Launcher grid.

Chrome Web Store

The Chrome Web Store contains a huge array of extensions to add to the Chrome browser to add all sorts of useful functionality, such as Google Translate, Grammarly, Google Dictionary, and Todoist. The store also offers a range of themes, apps, and simple games that can be added to Chrome.

Hot tip

Extensions can be found and managed by clicking the ✽ (jigsaw piece) icon at the top right of Chrome.

Installing an app from the Chrome Web Store

To install an app to add to Chrome:

1. Open the **Chrome Web Store** app from the Launcher, or search for it there.

2. Select the **Apps** category in the left panel of the store and scroll through the list of available apps, or search for one.

3. Click on an app to view details and user reviews. To install it, click the **Add to Chrome** button.

4. A dialog box will appear with permission details. Click on **Add app** to proceed. A download manager dialog will show installation progress. When done, the app icon will be added to the Launcher grid. You can also launch it from its Chrome Web Store page.

Using the Play Store

The Google Play Store enables you to install Android apps on your Chromebook, along with some PWAs – see page 150 for details.

Many apps are free to install (although some of these may feature in-app purchases – IAPs for short) while other (premium) apps cost money to download.

You can also purchase books, as well as movies and TV shows in the Play Store – which you can view in the Play Books and Google TV apps respectively.

Around the Play Store

Home screen options   Search box   Filter tabs   Play Points total

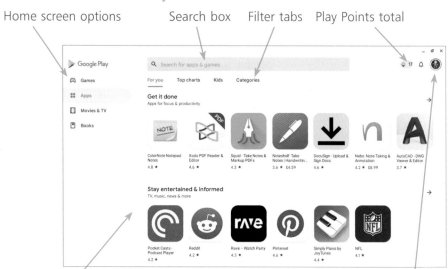

View and sort apps   Avatar

Hot tip

The charts are for Chromebook users, so may be different from those you will see on an Android smartphone.

- The Play Store's Home screen features options on the left for **Games**, **Apps**, **Movies & TV**, and **Books**. Clicking on one will show that type of content in the main panel. **Apps** is the default.

- You can click on the tabs near the top to filter what is shown in the main panel. For **Apps**, these are:

  For you. Suggested content based on your previous downloads and purchases, as well as your device.

  Top charts. See the most popular apps – top free, top grossing, and top paid, filterable by category.

Kids. Apps aimed at children; browsable by age range.

Categories. View apps from a host of categories, from Art & Design to Weather.

- Enter a term here to search for an app.
- Scroll down to view apps, sorted into different themes; click the **Right** arrow for one to see more examples.
- Click on your avatar to access more options, including **Manage apps & device** (where you can see installed/ purchased apps and available updates for them) and **Payments & subscriptions** (where you can add a payment method to buy apps and other content, and see any subscriptions you have).
- Your Play Points total. You can earn points for purchases of digital content, in-app items, and downloads from the Play Store. Use points to get discount coupons, in-app items, or Google Play credit.

Installing an app

Click on an app to see its description and user reviews. Then, click the **Install** button to install it. If it's a premium app, the button will say **Buy**, along with the price. You will need

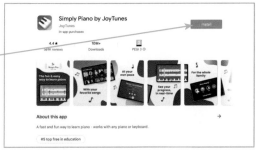

to have set up a payment method to purchase apps. The app will then be downloaded and installed on your Chromebook. Once ready, you can click the **Open** button to launch it (or **Play** if it's a game).

Play Protect

To prevent malware, Play Protect regularly checks your apps and devices for harmful behavior. You can do a manual scan by clicking on your avatar, selecting **Play Protect**, and then clicking the **Scan** button.

The **Games** screen has two extra tabs: **Events** (win prizes and rewards) and **Premium** (games to buy).

To add a payment method in **Payments & subscriptions**, click **Payment methods**, then add a credit/debit card, paysafecard, or PayPal account. You can also redeem a gift code in **Payments & subscriptions** to add credit to your account.

Apps and games can take up quite a bit of local storage space on your Chromebook.

Managing apps

Once you have installed some apps, you will want to keep tabs on which ones are installed, others you may have purchased previously but aren't downloaded to the Chromebook, and any updates available for your apps.

Viewing installed Play Store apps

To see apps installed via the Play Store:

1 Open the **Play Store** app from the Launcher, click on your account avatar image in the top-right corner, then select the **Manage apps & device** option.

2 The **Overview** tab of this screen shows any harmful apps detected, updates available, and the amount of local Chromebook storage used.

3 Click on the **Manage** tab to see a list of installed apps by default. Clicking on one

takes you to its Play Store page, where you can choose to **Uninstall** it (or **Update** it if an update is available).

4 Alternatively, check the boxes for any apps in the list you want to update or uninstall, then click the **Update** (if available) or **Uninstall** (trash can) icon at the top. If uninstalling, you will need to confirm.

Reinstalling apps

To reinstall apps previously bought or downloaded from the Play Store (on any device):

1 In the **Play Store** app, click on your avatar in the top-right corner, select **Manage apps & device**, then click the **Manage** tab to see a list of installed apps.

Hot tip

Only apps installed via the Play Store will be shown there. To manage other PWAs and apps from the Chrome Web Store, open the Settings app and go to **Apps** > **Manage your apps**.

154

2 Click on **Installed** and then select **Not installed**. The list will change to show apps in your Play Store library that aren't currently installed on your Chromebook.

3 Click on an app to go to its Play Store page and click **Install** to reinstall it.

4 Alternatively, check the boxes for any apps in the list that you want to reinstall, then click the **Install** icon at the top right.

Checking for app updates

To see available updates for installed apps, go to the **Overview** tab of the **Manage apps & device** screen.

Under **Updates available**, it will say how many updates are pending. Either click **Update all** or **See details** to see the apps and update them individually.

Automatic updates

To update your apps automatically, click on your avatar in the Play Store app and select **Settings**. Then, select **Network preferences** > **Auto-update apps** and select **Over any network** (or **Don't auto-update apps** if you want to disable automatic updates).

You can also enable/disable auto-update for individual apps by going to their Play Store page, clicking the **⋮** icon and checking or unchecking the box for **Enable auto update**.

Beware

Some apps you have installed previously on an Android phone may not be available for the Chromebook – a message will tell you this.

Hot tip

Some apps may be shared with up to five other members of a Family group. To set one up, tap your profile icon at the top right of the Play Store, then go to **Settings** > **Family** > **Sign up for Family Library**.

Using Android apps

Some Android apps are optimized for Chromebook, others appear as unaltered smartphone apps and may even appear in portrait (vertical) view, while some aren't available for Chromebook at all.

Controlling an Android app

As Android apps are designed to be used on a phone's touchscreen, it makes sense to use the touchscreen on your Chromebook to control them with taps and swipes,

particularly when playing fast-moving games. However, if you prefer, you can use the trackpad and pointer for most apps.

On-screen keyboard

While you can use the Chromebook's physical keyboard to type text in Android apps, this won't be usable if you are using a 2-in-1 Chromebook in tablet mode, with the screen

folded right over. In this case, an on-screen keyboard will appear when you tap on a field/option to type some text.

Closing an app

In a running Android app, move the pointer to the top of the screen to see the window controls at the top right. Click the **X** icon to close the app, or the — icon to minimize

the window – you can reopen it by clicking on the app icon on the Chrome OS desktop Shelf. Some apps also let you exit full-screen mode with the icon; you can then resize the window.

Hot tip

To take a screen grab in tablet mode, press the **Power** and **Volume-down** buttons (usually found on either side of your Chromebook) simultaneously.

Hot tip

In tablet mode, swipe from the top of the screen to enter **Overview** mode, showing all open apps. You can then click on the app's **X** icon to close it.

Google Play Pass

If you want to try out some premium apps and games but aren't sure about paying for them up front, Play Pass is your friend. Google's subscription service gives you access to a curated selection of hundreds of premium games and apps that would normally cost money to install.

As with other apps, you can install Play Pass apps on any of your Android-compatible devices. In addition, all the Play Pass content is free of any adverts and in-app purchases – all you have to pay is your monthly fee, or a yearly one.

Hot tip

As with many other apps, you can share Play Pass ones with your Family group.

Trying out Play Pass

To activate Play Pass for your account:

1 Open the **Play Store** app, click on your account avatar at the top right and select **Play Pass** from the menu.

2 On the screen that appears, click on **Get started**, then **Agree** to the terms of service.

Hot tip

To cancel your Play Pass subscription, click on your avatar in the Play Store and select **Payments & subscriptions** > **Subscriptions**. Click on **Google Play Pass**, then **Cancel subscription** at the bottom.

3 A dialog box will show you how much you will pay per month after a one-month free trial. You will need to have a payment method set up for your account. Scroll down and click on **Subscribe** to proceed, then enter your account password. You may be asked if you want to get updates about new games on Play Pass.

4 On the main Play Store screen, a new **Play Pass** category will have appeared at the top of the left panel. Clicking on it will reveal premium apps and games that you can now install and use for free (while you are a subscriber).

Beware

After you cancel Play Pass, you'll be able to continue using its apps until your subscription expires, but then you will lose access to them.

Play Games app

If you are an avid gamer, it's good to keep track of your own achievements and those of your friends. The Google Play Games app lets you do this and more.

Using Play Games
To use the Play Games app:

1 Open the **Play Games** app from the Launcher. It should be installed by default; if not, install it from the **Play Store** app.

2 If you haven't used Play Games before, you'll be asked to create a username and profile image – you can change these later.

3 The **Profile** screen shows your **Friends** and suggestions for others to invite – or you can get a link to send. Switching to the **Achievements** tab shows all of your gaming achievements. Click on one achievement to view it, then the game name at the top to view achievements and leaderboards for that game.

4 The **Home** screen shows the games you have been playing, along with suggestions for others to install.

5 The **Library** screen shows the games currently installed. Scroll to the right to also see a few built-in games you can play. Underneath is a list of previously downloaded games you may want to reinstall and play again.

158

11 Video Calling

Whether you want to keep
in touch with friends and
family or discuss business
with remote co-workers,
video calling is super-useful.
In this chapter, we take a
detailed look at Google Meet
and show you how to get
started with other popular
video-conferencing services.

Start using Google Meet

While most of the popular video-conferencing services can be used on the Chromebook, as we will explore later, we'll start with Google Meet as it is integrated with the Google Workspace apps such as Gmail, Contacts, and Calendar – and its meetings can also be started or joined from them.

Creating a meeting with Google Meet
To use Google Meet to start a meeting:

1 Open the **Google Meet** app from the Launcher. If it isn't there, go to **meet.google.com** in the Chrome web browser, click in the Omnibox, and select the ☕ **Install** icon on the right.

2 To create a meeting for others to join, click on **New meeting** and you will see three options:

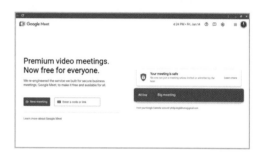

- **Create a meeting for later**. This will give you a link to share with others for a meeting at a later time. Don't forget to copy it yourself, by clicking the 🖿 icon, so that you don't lose it.
- **Start an instant meeting**. This immediately starts a new meeting to which you can invite others. See page 163 for how to add people to an existing meeting.
- **Schedule in Google Calendar**. This takes you to Google Calendar (in Chrome or the app) to create a scheduled event for the meeting; add a title, date and time; and invite guests. For more details on how to create a Calendar event, see page 131.

Joining a meeting in Google Meet
To join a created or scheduled Google Meet meeting, simply paste the link for it into the **Enter a code or link** box on the Google Meet home screen.

Hot tip

Upon joining your first Google Meet meeting, you will need to give permission for it to use your camera and microphone.

Starting or joining a meeting from other apps

You don't need to be in the Google Meet app, or on the website, to start or join a meeting. You can do so from several other Google Workspace apps:

- **Gmail**. In the Gmail app, you will find the **Meet** section at the bottom of the left panel. Click on **New meeting** to start one, or **Join a meeting** to join an existing one. Creating a new meeting creates a link for it and prompts you to share it with contacts by clicking **Send invite**, or just start the meeting straight away with **Start now**. If you are joining a meeting, you simply enter the link for it supplied by the organizer.

Hot tip

After clicking on the link to join a meeting, you get the chance to check your audio and video, and see who is already in the meeting, before clicking **Join now**.

- **Calendar**. In the **Calendar** app, create a scheduled event that has Google Meet video conferencing enabled and click the **Join with Google Meet** button. The event organizer will by default be the meeting host. To schedule your own meeting, create an event and click the **Add Google Meet video conferencing** button.

- **Contacts**. Go to **contacts.google.com** or click the **Contacts** icon in the sidebar of Gmail. Open a contact and click the **Start video call** icon to start an instant Google Meet meeting – click on the **Send email** button to invite them.

Hot tip

Scheduled meetings will also appear on the Google Meet home screen. Click on one to join it.

- **Chat**. Go to **chat.google.com**, open the **Chat** app (if installed), or select the **Chat** section in the left panel of

Gmail and start a text chat with a contact. Click on the **Add video meeting** icon at the bottom right, then the **Send message icon**. You can both now click on the **Video meeting** box in the chat to join it.

Don't forget

You can start a group conversation in **Google Chat** by clicking the **+** button next to **Spaces**. Then, you can share a Google Meet link with everyone in it.

Meeting controls

During a Google Meet meeting, you have access to a wide array of controls and options:

Around the Google Meet meeting interface

The code   Main controls   Person speaking   Additional controls

162

Hot tip

Depending on the options set by the meeting host, you may not be able to use certain features, whose icons will be dimmed.

Hot tip

If the host is using a business or education account, you may also see a **Raise hand** icon. Click it to "raise your hand" in the meeting, by adding a hand icon to your tile.

- The code (last part of its URL address, after **meet.google.com/**) for the meeting – or, if it's a Calendar event, the name for it.
- A blue border around someone's picture indicates that they are speaking. The layout of the participants' images can be altered. See page 164 for more details.
- The main controls for the meeting are:

  Turn microphone Off/On. When **Off**, it will appear red with a line through the icon.

  Turn camera Off/On. When **Off**, your Google account profile image/avatar will be shown instead of your camera feed.

  Turn captions Off/On. When **On**, participants' speech will be converted into text at the bottom of the screen.

  Present now. Start sharing your screen, a window, or a tab to present to the meeting – for more details, see page 166.

More options. This brings up a menu with extra options, including casting the meeting to another display, changing the on-screen layout, going full-screen, applying visual effects, and accessing the settings.

Leave call. Click this to leave the call. If you're the meeting host, you get the option to end the call for everyone or just leave and let the others continue chatting.

- Additional features and controls:

Meeting details. This shows the title and scheduled date/time for the meeting, along with the URL for it. Below that, any files attached to its Calendar event will be shown – click on one to go to its Google Drive link and view it.

People. The number by it shows the current number of participants. Click it to see a list of them. If you're the host, you can also mute everyone else and add people.

Chat with everyone. Clicking this brings up a panel where participants may send text messages. Type your message and then click the ▷ icon to send it.

Activities. This shows a panel with any activities available for the meeting. By default, only **Whiteboarding** will appear. You'll need to be using a Google Workspace business or education account to access other options such as **Breakout rooms**, **Q&A surveys**, **Polls**, and **Games**.

Host controls. This icon only appears for the meeting host (or co-host(s) if enabled via a business or education account). The menu contains settings to help the host keep control of the meeting. These include preventing other participants from sharing their screen, sending chat messages, and turning on their microphone and/or video. For more details, see page 167.

Hot tip

You can also access many options using keyboard shortcuts – see page 167 for more details.

Hot tip

You can also use the text chat feature to share links to files on Google Drive – see page 165 for more details.

Viewing options

Depending on how many people are in a Google Meet meeting, you may want to adjust the on-screen layout of participants. You can also blur your background or replace it with a different one.

Adjusting the screen layout

To change the layout of participants:

1 Click on the ⋮ icon at the bottom of the screen to bring up the **More options** menu.

2 Select the **Change layout** option from the menu. A dialog box will appear with four options:

Auto. This lets Google Meet choose a suitable layout for you.

Tiled. The standard tiled layout shows participants in equal-sized tiles in a grid – you can set the maximum number of tiles (up to 49) using the slider at the bottom of the dialog box.

Spotlight. Only show the active speaker, presentation, or person you have pinned (via the **People** icon).

Sidebar. The active speaker or presentation is shown in the main view, while others are shown in smaller tiles on the right.

Changing the background

To change the background for your camera view:

1 Click on the ⋮ icon at the bottom of the screen to bring up the **More options** menu.

2 Select the **Apply visual effects** option from the menu. Under **No effect & blur**, you can choose the blur level of your real background. Alternatively, you can replace it with one of the backdrops available in the **Backgrounds** section. Some of the backdrops are even animated.

Hot tip

You can add your own custom background by clicking the top-left icon under **Backgrounds** and uploading an image.

Messaging and sharing files

During a meeting, you can also exchange text messages with everyone else. This can be useful for spelling something out or sharing a link to a file.

Chatting with everyone
To send text messages to a group:

1 Click on the 🗩 icon at the bottom right. This brings up the **In-call messages** panel on the right of the screen, where you can view text messages from other participants in the meeting.

2 Type your message in the field at the bottom of the panel, then click the ▷ icon on the right to send it. It will then appear under other messages in the panel.

Sharing a file during a meeting
To share a file with everyone:

1 Click on the 🗩 icon to bring up the **In-call messages** panel.

2 To share your document, it will need to be on Google Drive. Copy its link from there, then paste it into the message field of the **In-call messages** panel.

Sharing a file before a meeting
Files can also be attached to a meeting's Calendar event (before the meeting or during it):

1 In the **Calendar** app, open the meeting event and click the pencil icon to edit it. Click the 🔗 **Add attachment** icon at the top of the description field.

2 Choose a file from Google Drive and click **Insert**. Click the **Save** button at the top and choose the permission level for the shared file(s), then click **Invite**.

Messages are shared with everyone in the meeting (or breakout room) – there is no way to chat privately with one person in Google Meet. To do that, you'd need to open a separate Google Chat session with them (see page 161).

see page 161

In-call messages   ×

Let everyone send messages

Messages can only be seen by people in the call and are deleted when the call ends.

You 12:04 PM
Hello everyone!

Jo, do you have that file to share?

Jo Bloggs 12:05 PM
No

You 12:05 PM
Ah, hold on. I think I have it here.

You 12:09 PM
https://docs.google.com/document/d/1XMWKbOM8eGlMR86CrnG93R9l3vzpr71QVfxlZZWxWtY/edit

Send a message to everyone   ▷

Files attached to the Calendar event can be found via the **Meeting details** menu in Meet.

The ability to share your screen may not be permitted by the meeting host, in which case the icon will be dimmed. Ask your host for permission to share.

Beware

Sharing your entire screen or the current browser window with the meeting in it can cause an "infinity mirror" effect, so it's best to share another window or tab.

Sharing your screen

During a meeting, you can present documents to others by sharing your screen: the entire screen, a window, or just a tab. Participants may also take part in a whiteboarding session.

Sharing your screen
To share your screen with everyone in the meeting:

1 Click on the [icon] **Present now** icon at the bottom of the screen. A menu will appear: choose to share your entire screen, a window, or a tab.

2 If sharing a window or tab, you will need to select one to share. Choose one from the menu and click the

Share button. If you don't want to share audio for the window/tab, uncheck **Share tab audio**.

3 Your own screen will switch to the shared tab, which others will be able to see in the meeting. You can also view

it (at a reduced size by default) within Google Meet. You can easily return to the tab view by clicking on **View tab** at the top. When you are finished presenting, click on **Stop sharing** or **Stop presenting** at the top of Google Meet.

Host options and shortcuts

The organizer of the meeting is by default the host, in charge of moderating it. For this purpose, there are a number of special options available to the host. In addition, all participants can use a range of handy keyboard shortcuts for certain functions.

Host options

Only the host can see the 🛡 **Host controls** icon in the bottom-right corner. Its options include:

Host management. This master option lets you control options available to other meeting participants. For instance, you can opt whether to let everyone do the following:

- **Share their screen.** If this is turned **Off**, they won't be able to use the **Present now** function.
- **Send chat messages.**
- **Turn on their microphone.**
- **Turn on their video.**

Keyboard shortcuts

Available to all participants, these keyboard shortcuts are a handy alternative to clicking on-screen icons:

Ctrl + **d**	Turn mic **On** or **Off**
Ctrl + **e**	Turn camera **On** or **Off**
c	Show or hide captions
Ctrl + **Alt** + **c**	Show or hide the chat window
Ctrl + **Alt** + **k**	Increase number of participant tiles
Ctrl + **Alt** + **j**	Decrease number of participant tiles
Ctrl + **Alt** + **p**	Show or hide participants
Ctrl + **Alt** + **m**	Minimize or expand your video
Ctrl + **Alt** + **h**	Raise your hand (if option available)
Ctrl + **Alt** + **s**	Announce who is speaking
Ctrl + **Alt** + **i**	Announce information about the room

The host can opt to end the meeting for everyone, after clicking the 🔴 **Leave call** icon.

The host can mute everyone from the **People** menu and also remove selected people from the meeting there.

Screen reader software is required for these last two shortcuts.

Video calling with Skype

Unusually for a video-conferencing service, Skype lets you not only join meetings as a guest, but also start them without needing to sign up for a free Microsoft Live account – although you may well want to do that anyhow.

Starting a Skype video call

To start a video call on Skype:

1 Open the **Chrome** web browser and enter **skype.com** in the Omnibox. Now, click on the **Create a free video call** button on the Skype website.

2 On the next screen, you can name your meeting and then click **Create a free video call** to start
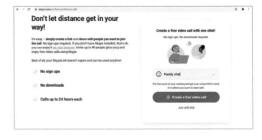
it. Or, you can click on **Join with link** to enter a link for a meeting sent to you by its organizer.

3 If you are starting a new meeting, you'll then see a link for it that you can share via email, or copy it and share by another means.

4 Click on **Start call** to begin the meeting. You'll need to allow Skype to use your microphone and camera (and, optionally, send notifications). Enter your name to use in the meeting. You can also **Invite** others to join.

5 You may still need to click on the **Camera** and **Mic** icons at the bottom to enable them during the meeting.

Hot tip

There is also a Skype Android app that you can install, but you'll need to sign up for an account to use it.

Hot tip

One interesting view option in Skype is **Together** mode, which places the guests' images together in a virtual scene.

Starting a Zoom meeting

Zoom is one of the most popular video-conferencing services available, and it's easy to use on your Chromebook. While you could use the website, the Zoom for Chrome PWA is recommended – available for free from the Play Store.

Starting a meeting
To start a meeting in the Zoom PWA:

1 Install **Zoom for Chrome – PWA** in the **Play Store** app, then open it from there or find its icon in the Chrome OS Launcher.

2 You'll see two options: **Join Meeting** and **Sign In**. You can join a meeting without needing an account – you just need the meeting ID, obtained from its organizer.

3 To start a new meeting, click **Sign In**. If you haven't yet got a Zoom account, you can sign in with your Google account: click on the **Google** icon at the bottom, choose an account, enter your date of birth (to verify you're over 16), then click the **Create Account** button.

4 On the Home screen, you can now **Join** a meeting, or **Schedule** one, or click **New Meeting** to start one instantly.

5 When the meeting screen appears, you'll be prompted to **Join Audio by Computer** – click the button so that you can hear sound during the meeting. Then, allow Zoom to use your microphone. Click on **Start Video** to allow it to use your camera.

Hot tip

For more help with Skype and Zoom, check out Video Chatting for Seniors in easy steps – view details at www.ineasysteps.com

Don't forget

You only need a Zoom account to start a new meeting, not to simply join one organized by someone else.

Microsoft Teams calls

Many businesses and schools use the Microsoft Teams communication platform, so you may well want to make a Teams video call on your Chromebook, as well as using its many other useful features, including the web-based Office suite.

Starting a Teams video conference
To start a Microsoft Teams meeting:

1 Open the **Chrome** app and, in the Omnibox, enter **microsoft.com/teams**
Sign in with a Microsoft Live account or sign up for a free account – you'll need to add a phone number to sign in to Teams to start a meeting.

2 After signing in, the main Teams menu gives options to **Invite people** to Teams, **Start chatting** via text messages, or **Meet now**. Click on the latter to start a video meeting.

3 Choose a name for the meeting and click on **Get a link to share** via email (or copy it to share another way). Then, click **Start meeting**.

4 Allow Teams to use your mic and camera, then choose your audio and video settings and click **Join now**.

5 During a meeting, you can invite more people: click the **People** icon, then add the name of a Teams contact, or click **Share invite** for options to share the meeting link.

12 Casting and Connecting

Sometimes you may want to connect your Chromebook to an external monitor, or cast its screen wirelessly to one. We also explore how to connect other devices and set up Phone Hub with your Android smartphone.

Casting your screen

If you have a Google Chromecast connected to a TV or monitor, or a Google Nest smart device or a smart TV, you can cast what's on your Chromebook's screen to it. You can cast the entire screen, a tab, app window, video, or file – or just audio to a speaker.

Casting the entire screen to another device

To quickly cast what's on your Chromebook's screen to another display:

1 On the Chrome OS desktop, click the Status Area at the bottom right of the Shelf to expand it.

2 To find the **Cast** option, you may have to swipe right with two fingers on the touchpad (or left on the screen) or click the second dot to show the second set of options.

3 Click the **Cast** option to see any compatible smart devices with a display on your Wi-Fi network. Select one to immediately start casting your entire screen to it.

4 A notification will appear above the Status Area to confirm that the screen is being cast. To stop casting, click **Stop** on the notification.

Casting a Chrome tab or file

To cast a Chrome browser tab, or a local file:

1 In the **Chrome** app, click the ⋮ icon at the top right and select **Cast** from the menu.

2 A list of devices available for casting will appear. Click on one to immediately start casting to it. The default option is to cast the current Chrome tab.

Don't forget

Google Docs, Sheets, and Slides documents appear in Chrome tabs, so can easily be cast to another screen. In the case of Slides, casting a tab will automatically take it into slideshow presentation mode.

3 To change what is cast, click the **Sources** option at the bottom of the **Cast** menu. You can choose to cast a tab, the desktop, or a file. Selecting the latter enables you to select a file – stored locally or on Google Drive – to cast.

4 To stop casting, click on the ⧉ **Cast** icon that has appeared at the top right of Chrome and then click on the device to which you are casting (indicated by a blue stop symbol to the left of its name).

Casting from an app

You can also cast the window, or video, from certain apps:

- In a PWA such as Twitter, YouTube, or Zoom, click on the ⋮ icon next to the window controls at the top right. Select **Cast...** to see identical options to those found in the Chrome browser so that you can choose a device and a source.

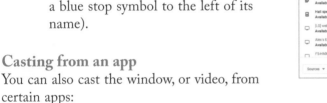

- Certain Android apps installed from the Play Store will allow you to cast from them. Look for the ⧉ **Cast** icon on the menu screen; it's usually at the top right, such as in the Google TV and Disney+ apps. Note that on some video-streaming apps, such as Netflix, it will only appear when you start playing a video. As before, click the ⧉ **Cast** icon and choose a device to stream to.

For more details on using video- and audio-streaming apps, see Chapter 9.

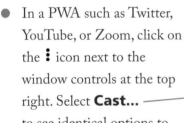

If you have a smart TV with an app from the same streaming service, you may be able to cast straight to it.

173

Using an external display

If you want to work on a larger display, you can connect your Chromebook to an external monitor or TV. The latter can be used to "mirror" the Chromebook's screen for an identical copy, or as a second desktop to view different things.

Connecting a display

Depending on the display's input ports, you will need a suitable cable to connect your Chromebook's video output port to it.

While some monitors feature a USB-C video input, most (and TVs) will have an HDMI port. Some Chromebooks have an HDMI output on the side; others have a USB-C port (which may double up as the mains power/charging port).

In the latter case, with an HDMI monitor, you will need a USB-C to HDMI cable – or you could use a standard HDMI cable coupled with a USB-C to HDMI adaptor.

Using a suitable cable/adaptor, it is also possible to connect a Chromebook to a monitor with a DisplayPort, DVI, or VGA input port.

So, before buying a cable and/or adaptor, check the video ports on both the monitor and your Chromebook to make sure you get the right connection.

Mirroring the built-in display

As soon as you connect the external display, by default it should show exactly what's currently being shown on your Chromebook's own built-in display. This is known as "mirroring".

However, it is possible to switch the view mode so that the external display shows a different screen from the one on the Chromebook's own display. This is great for multitasking, such as using one screen to do research on the internet or look at documents, while writing notes on the other screen.

You can even determine how the screens are arranged to alter how you move your touchpad cursor between them to navigate.

Don't forget

HDMI = High-Definition Multimedia Interface

USB = Universal Serial Bus

DVI = Digital Visual Interface

VGA = Video Graphics Array

Don't forget

If using a TV, make sure it is switched to the appropriate HDMI input to which the Chromebook is connected.

Hot tip

It's best to connect the cable to the monitor first, then the other end to your Chromebook. Otherwise, the Chromebook may not recognize the display has been connected.

Switching to an extended desktop

To make the external display show a different screen from the one on the Chromebook:

1 Open the **Settings** app and go to **Device** > **Displays**.

2 Here, you will see the current screen arrangement. By default, when you first connect an external monitor, it will mirror the Chromebook's display. To change this, uncheck the box for **Mirror Built-in display**.

3 You'll now see two separate rectangles in the **Displays** menu. By dragging and dropping them, you can change the screen arrangement. This determines how you navigate between them with the touchpad: for example, if the external display is placed on top of the built-in one, you move the pointer up from the latter to the former to reach it.

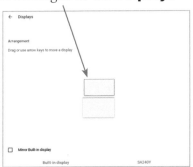

4 By selecting the external monitor in the **Displays** menu, you can alter its settings, including **Display size** (for icons, etc.), **Resolution**, and even **Orientation** (useful if you have a monitor that can rotate into portrait mode).

5 You can make the external monitor the main display: for the **Screen** option, click on the **Extended display** drop-down menu and change it to **Primary display**. To change it back, select the built-in display in the **Displays** menu and use the same **Screen** option.

Don't forget

You can find the **Settings** app in the Launcher, or you can click the **Status Area** and then the ⚙ icon there.

Hot tip

The **Overview** mode (accessed by pressing the key or swiping up with three fingers) shows both screens' previews for each desk. Switching desks will switch both screens to that desk.

Don't forget

Instead of using a wired connection, you can cast your screen (or a tab) to an external display connected to a Chromecast device.

Setting up Phone Hub

Chrome OS's Phone Hub feature enables you to connect your Chromebook to an Android smartphone to access some very useful features such as using its Wi-Fi hotspot.

Connecting your Android phone

To connect your phone, if you haven't already done so:

1 On your Chromebook, go to **Settings** > **Connected devices** and click **Set up** for the **Android phone** option.

2 Select your phone from the drop-down menu, click **Accept & continue**, then enter your Google account password to confirm. Your

phone will now be connected and you can use the **Smart Lock** feature to unlock your Chromebook with your phone.

With **Smart Lock** enabled, you won't need to enter a password when signing in to your account on the Chromebook – just unlock your phone.

176

Using Phone Hub features

With the phone connected, Phone Hub should be turned on by default, and its ▣ icon will appear on the right of the Shelf. Click on it there and you will see the following options:

- **Enable hotspot**. Turn this option **On** to use the phone's internet connection – handy if the Wi-Fi is down. You may see a message on your phone screen to get verification from your network provider – some operators may block this feature. Once it's set up, clicking **Enable hotspot** again will connect you to your phone's network after a few seconds.

- **Silence phone**. Mutes the sound on your phone.

- **Locate phone**. Click this and the phone should start sounding a loud alert, enabling you to find it.

- **Recent Chrome tabs**. These are from your phone; click on one to open it in Chrome on the Chromebook.

Setting up notifications

This optional Phone Hub feature enables you to receive notifications from your phone on your Chromebook. To set it up:

1 In the **Phone Hub** icon menu, click on **Set up**, then **Get started**.

2 A prompt will now appear on your phone's screen; click on **Turn on notifications** there and select the apps for which you want to receive notifications. Note: you must turn on **Google Play Services** for it to work; then, click **Done** on the Chromebook.

Beware

Be careful only to use trusted apps with the notifications feature. You will need to **OK** each one individually when setting it up.

Setting up text messaging

With this feature enabled, you can view and respond to your phone's text messages from your Chromebook. To set this up:

1 In the **Phone Hub** icon menu, click on the ⚙ icon to go to the settings. Click on the **Set up** button for the **Messages** option, then **Get started**.

2 Follow the instructions on your phone screen to complete the setup. You'll need to use its camera to scan a QR code shown on your Chromebook screen.

3 The **Messages** app will open on your Chromebook, where you can view all of your phone's text messages and respond to them.

Hot tip

With the **Messages** feature enabled, you can also video-call contacts using the Google Duo app on your Chromebook.

177

Connecting devices

At some point, you may well want to connect an external device – such as a mouse, external storage drive, or headphones – to your Chromebook. There are two main ways to do this: via a USB port or a wireless Bluetooth connection.

Connecting a USB device
Connecting and using a USB device is usually very simple: plug it in and it should work straight away.

Connecting a wireless printer
If you have a wireless printer connected to the same Wi-Fi network, the Chromebook should detect it automatically and it will be selectable in the drop-down menu for **Destination** when you print something (**Ctrl** + **p**). If not, go to **Settings** > **Print and scan**, where you can search for it or add it manually.

Pairing a Bluetooth device
To connect a wireless Bluetooth device:

1. Put your Bluetooth device into **Pairing** mode (check its manual to discover how to do so).

2. On the Chromebook, click at the bottom right to expand the Status Area, then click on the arrow under the **Bluetooth** icon.

3. It will now scan for nearby devices. When it finds the one you want to connect, click on it to commence

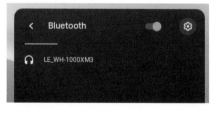

pairing. After a few seconds, the device should be paired successfully and can then be used.

4. If you want to disconnect the device, perhaps to use it with another computer or phone, go to **Settings** > **Bluetooth**, click the ⋮ icon next to the device and choose **Disconnect**. Only select the **Remove from list** option here if you want to unpair the device.

Don't forget

When finished with a connected USB drive, make sure to click the **Eject** icon next to its name in the Files app and wait a couple of seconds before removing the device.

Don't forget

Once paired, the Bluetooth device will be recognized in future and can be connected easily.

13 Maintenance and Troubleshooting

Keep your Chromebook's operating system up-to-date for the latest features, adjust its many settings, free up storage space, prolong its battery life, and keep it nice and clean.

Updating Chrome OS

It's important to keep your Chromebook's operating system up-to-date, not just to gain access to the latest features but also to keep it secure from malware and other threats.

Automatic updates

Your Chromebook will automatically check for updates to Chrome OS and download them when connected to the internet.

When this happens, you will see an **Update available** notification above the Status Area. Click on it and select **Restart to update**. The Chromebook will restart and install the update.

Checking for updates manually

You can also check manually whether a new Chrome OS update is available and, if so, install it.

1 With the Chromebook connected to the internet, open the **Settings** app and select **About Chrome OS** at the bottom of the left-hand panel.

2 Click the **Check for updates** button and the Chromebook will search online for an update. If it finds one, it will download it and start updating your device.

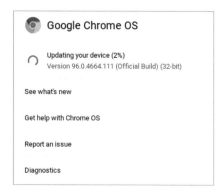

Google Chrome OS

Updating your device (2%)
Version 96.0.4664.111 (Official Build) (32-bit)

See what's new

Get help with Chrome OS

Report an issue

Diagnostics

3 When it has finished, click on **Restart** and the Chromebook will restart and install the update.

Testing experimental features

By default, Chrome OS updates are set to the "stable" channel, which means they are fully tested by Google. You can test more experimental new features by switching to the "beta" channel (low risk) or "dev" channel (higher risk).

To switch software channels, go to **Settings** > **About Chrome OS**, and select **Additional details**. Click on **Change channel** and choose one.

Don't forget

Every Chromebook has an Auto Update Expiry (AUE) date, after which it will no longer receive system software updates from Google. To check your AUE, go to **Settings** > **About Chrome OS** > **Additional details**, and look under **Update schedule**.

Beware

Back up any important files before switching to the dev channel. Switching back to the stable or beta channel requires a "powerwash", which will delete all locally stored data.

Adjusting system settings

The **Settings** app enables you alter a wide variety of system settings for your Chromebook to tailor it to your personal preferences and needs.

Settings categories

The left-hand panel of the **Settings** app offers the following options:

- **Network**. Here, you can check your Wi-Fi connection (and mobile data if your Chromebook supports it).
- **Bluetooth**. Turn it **On** or **Off** and check connected devices.
- **Connected devices**. See a connected phone and enable features such as **Smart Lock** and **Phone Hub**. The **Nearby Share** option lets you share data with a nearby device via Bluetooth.
- **Accounts**. See the currently signed in account(s), manage Google services syncing, and set up parental controls.
- **Device**. Alter settings for the touchpad, keyboard, display(s), storage management, and power (sleep options).
- **Personalization**. Change your account image, wallpaper, and screen saver (which shows when the screen is idle).
- **Search and Assistant**. Choose the preferred search engine, and adjust settings for Google Assistant voice control.
- **Security and privacy**. Alter lock screen and sign-in options (password only, or PIN or password). Manage other people, including enabling/disabling guest browsing and limiting sign-in to existing users.
- **Apps**. Manage your installed apps (including uninstalling) and their notification settings. You can also opt whether to restore running apps upon restarting the Chromebook.
- **Advanced**. Extra settings to alter date and time, languages and inputs, files, printers and scanners; turn on the Linux development environment; and manage accessibility features. The powerwash option will remove all accounts and reset your Chromebook to be just like new – only do so if you have a serious technical issue or want to sell or gift the Chromebook.
- **About Chrome OS**. Check for system updates.

For more information on Phone Hub features, see pages 176-177.

Aimed at software developers, the Linux development environment enables you to run Linux tools, editors, and IDEs (integrated development environments for programming).

For easier access to accessibility options, turn **On** the **Always show accessibility options** in the system menu option in **Settings** > **Advanced Accessibility**. This will add a new **Accessibility** icon to the Status Area panel so that you can access all of its options from there.

Accessibility features

Your Chromebook has built-in accessibility features. Enable and manage them in the **Settings** app, in the **Advanced** > **Accessibility** section. Here, we take a look at the key features.

Text-to-Speech options

- **Enable ChromeVox**. Your Chromebook's built-in screen reader gives spoken feedback on windows, menus, and selected text or items. Turn it **On/Off** with **Ctrl** + **Alt** + **z**.
- **Enable select-to-speak**. Highlight what you want to hear, then press (Q or ◉) + **s**.
- **Text-to-Speech voice settings**. Adjust Text-to-Speech options such as speech properties and voice type/language.

Display options

- **Use high contrast mode**. This inverts the screen colors to make it easier to read text. Turn it **On/Off** with **Ctrl** + (Q or ◉) + **h**.
- **Enable screen magnifier**. Navigate with the touchpad, or **Ctrl** + **Alt** + arrow keys. Turn it **On/Off** with **Ctrl** + (Q or ◉) + **m**.
- **Enable docked magnifier**. This shows a magnified view, at the top of the screen of the area around the touchpad pointer.

Keyboard and text input

- **Enable sticky keys**. To type shortcuts sequentially.
- **Enable on-screen keyboard**. When you select a text field, a keyboard appears along the bottom of the screen.
- **Enable dictation**. Press (Q or ◉) + **d** and you can then type with your voice.
- **Switch Access**. Control the Chromebook with one or two (USB or Bluetooth) switches or keys.

Mouse and touchpad

- **Automatically click when the cursor stops**. As soon as you stop moving the pointer, it will click the item it's on.
- **Highlight the mouse cursor when it's moving**. This puts a red circle around the pointer when you're moving it.

Audio and captions

- **Captions**. See live captions (subtitles) for media in the Chrome browser.

Freeing up storage space

While most of your Chromebook's files and data will be stored online, in Google Drive and other cloud services, its local storage may soon fill up if you download large files or install a lot of apps.

If your local storage is near full, you may encounter issues with downloading files, loading web pages, saving settings, adding new user accounts, and using Android apps.

Checking and manage storage

To see how much of your Chromebook's local storage has been used and access options to free up space:

1 Open the **Settings** app, select **Device** in the left panel, and click on **Storage management**.

2 At the top, you'll see how much of your storage is in use or available. Below this are several options to help you free up space:

- **My files**. Click this to open your **My files** folder in the **Files** app. Delete any files you don't need any more.

- **Browsing data**. This takes you to the **Clear browsing data** option in the Chrome app, with **Cached images and files** selected. Click the **Clear data** button to delete them.

- **Apps and extensions**. Click this to go to the **Manage your apps** setting. Here, you will see a list of all installed apps. Click on one to see its details, with the option to **Uninstall** it.

- **Other users**. This takes you to the **Manage other people** setting. You can remove a user by clicking the **X** by their name.

- **System**. This isn't an option, but shows the amount of storage used by Chrome OS. You can't reduce this.

- **External storage preferences**. Any connected USB storage drives will show up here, and you can toggle their switches **On** to allow Google Play Store apps to read and write files on them.

Hot tip

Upload files to Google Drive and then delete them from your local storage (in **My files**) to save space.

Prolonging battery life

Like any laptop computer, your Chromebook will need to be plugged into mains power every now and then to recharge its battery. Find out ways to keep it running on the battery longer and prolong the battery's life.

Checking battery level

Hover the pointer over the battery icon in the Status Area at the bottom right to see the exact percentage and approximate time remaining before it runs out.

For more details, go to **Settings** > **About Chrome OS** > **Diagnostics**.

This will also show the battery health percentage, which will eventually decline with usage. You can also click **Run Discharge test** to check for problems.

Conserving power

Ways to save power when running on the battery:

- Lower the screen brightness with the (small) ☼ key – and the keyboard backlight, if you have one, with the ☼ key.
- Close unused apps and Chrome browser tabs.
- Turn off Bluetooth when not needed, by clicking on its icon in the Status Area. You could even turn off Wi-Fi if you are able to work offline and don't currently need an internet connection.
- Go to **Settings** > **Device** > **Power** and ensure the **When idle** options are set to **Sleep** (and also when the cover is closed).

Battery care

To help prolong your battery's long-term health:

- Avoid letting it run out of juice completely. It's advisable to start recharging it when it gets below 20%.
- Don't let your Chromebook run too hot, as this could cause both the CPU and battery to overheat. Keep it away from strong sunlight and heating outlets. Also, keep it well ventilated.

Don't forget

You can set Google Drive documents to be available offline so that you can continue working on them when Wi-Fi is turned **Off** or unavailable. See pages 110-111 for more details on working offline.

Cleaning your Chromebook

You will no doubt want to keep your Chromebook looking new and shiny, but careful cleaning is required to avoid potential damage to the screen and electronics.

Cleaning the screen

Your Chromebook screen is bound to gather dust and fingerprints – particularly if you use the touchscreen a lot. To avoid scratches and damage, only use certain materials to clean it:

Beware

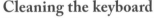

- A soft, clean lint-free cloth, of the type you would use to clean eyeglasses or camera lenses.
- To remove any stubborn marks, use an alcohol-free cleaning fluid recommended for computer screens, but make sure the Chromebook is turned **Off** and don't spray directly onto the screen.
- Alternatively, use screen wipes that are recommended for use on computer screens.

Always wipe the screen carefully and use appropriate materials to avoid potential damage. If in doubt, check your Chromebook manufacturer's guidance.

Cleaning the keyboard

Over time, dust and crumbs may gather in gaps between keys and the body of the Chromebook. Turning the computer upside down and giving it a shake may remove some of the debris. Alternatively, use an "air duster" to squirt compressed air into gaps around the keys.

Troubleshooting issues

While your Chromebook should run smoothly for the most part, you may sometimes come across an issue. Here, we look at a few of the most common problems and how to fix them.

Hardware issues

- **Bluetooth doesn't work**. Make sure the other device is supported, charged, and near enough to the Chromebook. If that doesn't work, try turning Bluetooth **Off** and then **On** again.
- **Keyboard doesn't work**. If you are using a 2-in-1 convertible Chromebook, make sure the screen isn't rotated more than 180°; otherwise, it will switch to tablet mode. If the keyboard still isn't working, try powering the Chromebook **Off** and **On** again.
- **Touchpad doesn't work**. Again, if using a 2-in-1 convertible Chromebook, make sure the screen is rotated less than 180°. Or, try drum-rolling your fingers on the touchpad, pressing the **Esc** key repeatedly, or powering the Chromebook **Off** and **On** again.
- **Touchscreen doesn't work**. Check for dust or dirt on the screen and wipe it off carefully (see page 185). Alternatively, power the Chromebook **Off** and **On** again.
- **Battery not charging**. Check that your charger cable is connected properly to both the Chromebook and the wall socket. If you still have a problem, unplug the charger from both, then plug it back into the Chromebook first, then the wall socket.

System issues

- **Chromebook crashes or freezes**. Close all apps and browser windows, then power the Chromebook **Off** and **On** again. If you still have a problem, try uninstalling any new apps or extensions. Or, use the **Diagnostics** setting to run a memory test.
- **Chromebook is slow**. Use the **Diagnostics** setting to check CPU usage and run some tests.
- **Chromebook keeps restarting or "Chrome OS is missing or damaged" error message appears**. Try using **Diagnostics** to run a memory test. If there is still an issue, you may need to "powerwash" your Chromebook to do a factory reset. If that fails, you may need to "recover" it; this involves removing and reinstalling Chrome OS, so is not a step to be taken lightly.

If a system update fails to download or brings up an error, try turning the Chromebook **Off** and **On**. If that doesn't work, you may need to do a powerwash or recovery.

Doing a powerwash or recovery of your Chromebook will delete all locally stored files and data, so back them up to an external drive if possible.